EMPOWERMENT SKILLS FOR LEADERS

A COMPONENT OF THE NATIONAL FAMILY DEVELOPMENT CREDENTIAL™ PROGRAM

INSTRUCTOR MANUAL

Claire Forest, PhD

Katie Palmer-House EdD

Carol West, MA

Copyeditor: Robert Kulik
Illustrator: Camille Doucet
Graphic Designer: Tina Field Howe

Third Edition

© 2020 Claire Forest

Forest Home Press LLC

A Word about Copyright

National FDC Director Claire Forest owns the copyright to all the National Family Development Credential Program publications, including *Empowerment Skills for Family Workers* and its accompanying *Instructors Manual* and *Portfolio Advisor Manual,* as well as *Empowerment Skills for Leaders* and its accompanying *Instructor Manual,* all FDC exams and protocols, and all forms used in the management of the Family Development Credential program and on the FDC website: www.familydevelopmentcredential.org.

A copyright protects an author (or program developer) from others claiming that original author's work as their own, or from inserting bits and pieces of that work into their own without permission or proper attribution. Thus, the copyright protects the original work from being misrepresented. In the context of the current work, it helps ensure that people who earn the Family Development Worker's Credential or the Family Development Leadership Credential have studied the genuine and authentic course.

How do I share what I've learned?

If you want to share what you've learned, you have several options; for example, you could:

1. Offer a short workshop. If you copy a handout, leave the copyright and source statements intact.

2. Write an article, including short quotes from this book, with proper attribution, for example: "From Claire Forest, Empowerment Skills for Leaders (Forest Home Press, 2020)."

3. When citing quotations, include the relevant page number(s).

Email Claire at cnd3@cornell.edu or Amy Knight at nationalfdc@uconn.edu with any questions that you have about using the curriculum.

Acknowledgements

There are many people to thank as we complete this update of the FDC leadership curriculum. We greatly appreciate the insights and suggestions from a group of experienced and talented FDC instructors who facilitate *Empowerment Skills for Leaders*. They are Rosalyn Ferguson (New York City), Haley Scott (Connecticut Office of Early Childhood, Hartford, CT), Caroline Mavridis (Center for the Study of Culture, Health & Human Development, University of Connecticut), Erica Henry (Washington, DC), Sonya Montoya (Flagstaff, AZ) and Angela Zimmerman (Molloy College, Long Island, NY). Angela and her team also compiled an extensive list of relevant articles to supplement as additional resources and suggested material for the updated curriculum.

In addition, a special thank you goes to Angela Zimmerman, Lisa Miller, and Sherry Radowitz (Molloy College) for pioneering the adaptation of *Empowerment Skills for Leaders* for the higher-education audience. While the curriculum was initially developed for leaders and supervisors in the human services field, Angela and her colleagues recognized how beneficial it would be for leaders within the various departments of the college. To this end, they facilitated several cohorts of department leaders and college administrators—and with great success. In the summer of 2019, National FDC collaborated with Molloy College to hold its first *Empowerment Skills for Leaders* Instructors Training Institute specifically for those in higher education, with representatives from several different colleges and universities participating.

It was a great pleasure to again work with Camille Doucet, the skillful artist and illustrator of *Empowerment Skills for Family Workers*, who sketched the cover and text illustrations for the first edition of *Empowerment Skills for Leaders*. You will see her "peripheral vision" sketch in this updated edition.

We are also grateful to our former colleagues at Cornell University's College of Human Ecology and Cornell Cooperative Extension for the opportunity to collaborate in promoting the principles and practice of family development that foster healthy families and caring communities. Since 2011, this collaboration has continued with our colleagues, Dr. Charlie Super and Dr. Sara Harkness, in the Center for the Study of Culture, Health & Human Development, Department of Human Development and Family Sciences at the University of Connecticut.

To our own families, we send our deepest thanks for your gifts of love, now and always. As you nurture and inspire us to realize our own empowerment potential, you teach us the meaning of love.

Claire, Katie, and Carol

About the Authors

Claire Forest, PhD

Claire is Assistant Professor in the University of Connecticut's Department of Human Development and Family Studies, where she directs the National Family Development Credential Program. In 2016, the Federal Office of Head Start approved the National Family Development Credential for fulfillment of requirements under section (1302,91 e) (7) of the Head Start Performance Standards, Staff Qualifications and Competency. Claire especially appreciated this recognition, as it represented the fulfillment of her mentor Urie Bronfenbrenner's vision.

Prior to moving to the University of Connecticut, Claire was a faculty member of Cornell University's Department of Human Development (1981–2010). She directed the Cornell Empowering Families Project, which developed and administered the Family Development Credential Program until 2010, when the program moved to the University of Connecticut. She has authored many publications, including the FDC curriculum—*Empowerment Skills for Family Workers*, the first edition of which was published in 1995. She also authored a 1995 monograph entitled *Credentialing Caregivers* and commissioned by the Harvard Family Research Project.

From 1981 to 1991, Claire served as Training and Dissemination Director of the Cornell Family Matters Project, overseeing national implementation. Before joining Cornell, Claire directed a day-care center and family resource center. She is widely respected as a leader in the field of family support and engagement.

Katie Palmer-House, EdD

Katie was Senior Trainer of the Cornell Empowering Families Project from 2000 to 2010. Before joining Cornell, she was an FDC instructor and portfolio advisor in Dutchess County, NY, and worked as a frontline family support supervisor and deputy director of a community action agency. During her years with National FDC, Katie made many important contributions, especially to *Empowerment Skills for Leaders*, including the section on learning styles, which is included in this edition. Her research focused on adult and community education, and teaching practices that foster transformative learning.

Carol West, M.A.

Carol joined the National FDC team in 2011 as the Senior Trainer and Portfolio Reviewer. Prior to her consulting work with FDC, Carol had a long career with Cornell University Cooperative Extension in Jefferson County, NY. During her tenure with Cooperative Extension, her educational focus included youth development, parenting education, child care, and family engagement.

Carol was also Director of a statewide Parental Information and Resource Center, the goal of which was to assist schools and community agencies to more effectively engage parents in their children's education. In addition, she was an instructor and portfolio advisor for both *Empowerment Skills for Family Workers* and *Empowerment Skills for Leaders*, teaching several classes over the years.

INTRODUCTION

Welcome to the Empowerment Skills for Leaders curriculum!

A brief history of the Family Development Credential (FDC)

Empowerment Skills for Leaders is a component of the comprehensive curriculum of the National Family Development Training and Credentialing (FDC) Program initially developed by the Cornell Empowering Families Project at Cornell University in the mid-1990s. Since 2010, the program has been administered by the University of Connecticut. The core component of the curriculum, *Empowerment Skills for Family Workers: A Worker Handbook*, was written by National FDC Director Claire Forest as part of a major New York State Initiative to develop a family-centered, strengths-based, professional development training program for frontline family workers.

Empowerment Skills for Leaders was initially developed for family support professionals interested in supervising and leading their organizations using the principles and practices of the Family Development approach. However, both curricula have expanded their audience to include professionals from a variety of different fields, including business and higher education.

The National Family Development Credential (FDC) Program has been pioneering a paradigm shift from the "deficit" family support model to an "empowerment-based" model since the mid-1990s. In 1990, the New York State Council on Children and Families called together fifteen major state agencies to talk about a new approach built on family strengths.

The New York Department of State's Community Services Block Grant Program, directed by Evelyn Harris, took a leadership role among the state agencies. The Department of State, through its statewide Community Action Agencies, had been experimenting with shifting its paradigm to a "family development" model. They invited Cornell University's Empowering Families Project into the discussion, because of Cornell's exemplary work in training human service workers in empowerment skills. The state agencies agreed that an interagency training and credentialing program for agency workers should be developed, beginning with front-line workers, and later offering specialized training to agency supervisors and state agency staff. The New York Department of State provided initial funding and selected Cornell to develop the FDC curriculum *Empowerment Skills for Family Workers*, train and oversee FDC facilitators, and establish a permanent training and credentialing system.

In 2010, the FDC program moved to the University of Connecticut, which now provides administrative oversight and issues the FDC credentials. National FDC Director Claire Forest continued her leadership throughout the transition. Thousands of agencies and organizations nationwide have adopted a strengths-based paradigm using the Family Development Credential curriculum.

How this program differs from other programs

Empowerment Skills for Leaders is a professional development training for supervisors and leaders interested in using empowerment-based leadership in their agencies, businesses, or educational institutions. Leaders who already have FDC-credentialed staff in their organization will be able to enhance their organization's capacity for providing empowerment-based support using the same principles and practices that their family workers use with families. Leaders who are unfamiliar with FDC will learn practical ways to build their organizational capacities in areas of empowerment-based supervision, interagency collaboration, strengths-based assessment, multicultural competence, and personal self-empowerment.

Empowerment Skills for Leaders differs from traditional leadership development trainings in the following ways:

- It is designed to help leaders build on specific skills and competencies they already have, and that workers have learned through strengths-based family development training. Most leadership training programs provide information about ways to use generic strategies in all-purpose situations.

- *It provides an in-depth, interactive, and reflective program that encourages personal and organizational transformation.* Leadership trainings are often conducted in one-day, or time-intensive, large-group seminars with little or no time for open discussion or personal reflection.

- It was developed for all levels of leadership in organizations, from board members and executive directors to frontline supervisors. Most leadership programs are created for executive management or top administrators who then become responsible for implementing organizational change.

- It helps leaders identify the areas where empowerment-based change within the organization can begin to make meaningful differences in family support programs and agency-based outcomes. Most leadership programs focus on teaching motivational techniques designed to increase staff productivity without understanding that policies and practices of the organization may also need to change for families to accomplish goals, and for agencies to achieve outcomes.

- It promotes networking and collaboration among participants in a positive learning environment to support their collective goals. Most leadership programs focus on the individual and not as much on partnering with other professionals.

How Empowerment Skills for Leaders was developed

Empowerment Skills for Leaders (ESFL) was first published in 2002. It was developed over a year and a half, involving focus-group research with FDC-credentialed supervisors and other community leaders, as well as curriculum reviews and pilot testing of training activities. Many of the activities in this course were field tested in leadership pilot programs and found to be useful in starting or advancing discussion about empowerment-based leadership. Experienced ESFL instructors also suggested new topics to include in updating this new edition.

Developing the *Empowerment Skills for Leaders* Handbook and the accompanying Instructors Manual has been an iterative process, reflecting the thoughtful feedback of instructors, participants, and curriculum reviewers. We are grateful for their conscientious and gracious assistance.

Criteria for becoming an *Empowerment Skills for Leaders* instructor

Empowerment Skills for Leaders translates the core components and practices of empowerment-based family support presented in the *Empowerment Skills for Family Workers* curriculum within the context of relationships and mission of family-serving organizations. For this reason, *Empowerment Skills for Leaders* instructors need to have a good understanding of the *Empowerment Skills for Family Workers* concepts and the FDC credentialing process. Experienced FDC instructors with two or more years of supervisory experience are strong candidates. A master's degree in education, psychology, social work, or a related field is also required; however, years of experience will also be considered.

Prospective leadership instructors submit applications to attend an FDC Leadership Instructor's Training Institute that describe their past supervisory and group facilitation experience, and their reasons for wanting to become a leadership instructor. Upon acceptance, they attend a 2.5-day train-the-trainer institute. Leadership instructors are also required to attend a National FDC–led Update at least once every three years to remain active. Most recently, FDC Updates are presented as webinars and are offered at least once a year.

The Leadership Credential

Requirements for receiving the National Family Development Leadership Credential administered by the University of Connecticut are:

- Attendance to all sessions of the 30-hour *Empowerment Skills for Leaders* course facilitated by a certified National FDC instructor.
- Development of a Leadership Portfolio—which applies the concepts of empowerment-based leadership—by working with a "peer advisor."

Leadership Portfolio

The FDC Leadership Portfolio is a compilation of skills practices and reflections demonstrating a leader's understanding and practice of empowerment-based leadership. Portfolios are developed throughout the course. Leaders work with one another for each chapter, serving as peer advisors and providing verbal and written feedback.

Components of the Leadership Portfolio are:

- One *Independent Learning Project for each of the five chapters*. Suggestions for projects are listed at the end of each chapter, but leaders are encouraged to develop their own projects relevant to their workplace.
- One *Leadership Empowerment Plan* that identifies a short-term goal and outlines the steps to achieve it. Leaders reflect on their own strengths and challenges, applying the concepts learned in this course.
- An *Overall Reflection* at the end of the course that summarizes what they have learned, initial results of their Leadership Empowerment Plan, and how they will continue to implement the skills and concepts of empowerment-based leadership.

Peer Advisors

Peer advisors assist other leaders attending the course with support and feedback on the development of their leadership portfolio. A peer advisor helps their advisee with the following:

1. Providing support in developing an Independent Learning Project for each chapter, and a Leadership Empowerment Plan that is meaningful and manageable.

2. Affirming the project involves an activity that demonstrates how they have practiced some of the concepts presented in each chapter.

3. Brainstorming opportunities and challenges that may arise during the project and discussing how they might handle them.

4. Arranging time to review and discuss each Independent Learning Project and the Leadership Empowerment Plan.

5. Providing verbal and written strength-based feedback that identifies the leader's strengths and possible suggestions for future actions. A secondary role of feedback is to practice and enhance skills at offering strength-based feedback to their own workers and staff.

The group can make a collective decision on whether to work with the same advisor for each chapter or not. We recommend leaders work with different advisors for each chapter to receive a wider range of feedback and perspectives.

Completed portfolios are submitted by the instructor to National FDC for review. Upon approval, the FDC Leadership Credential is issued by the University of Connecticut.

College Credit and Contact Hours

College credit for earning the FDC Leadership Credential is available. For the most up-to-date information on number of credits and fees, contact the National FDC Program Manager at nationalfdc@uconn.edu or check the FDC website (www.familydevelopmentcredential.org) for information and application forms.

Contact hours (Continuing Education Units) are also available. Participants can receive contact hours for each hour they attend the course. Sign-in/sign-out sheets from the instructor are submitted with the application.

Application forms for both college credit and contact hours are on the FDC website.

Offering Empowerment Skills for Leaders in your community

Empowerment Skills for Leaders is intended to be offered in community-based settings or large institutions where supervisors and leaders learn while they do informal outreach, networking and relationship building that may lead to future interagency or interdepartmental partnerships and collaborations. Building on your current network of interagency or interdepartmental contacts is a good way to promote and market the course. Agencies who have FDC-credentialed workers are also a good place to start by informing their supervisors and leaders about the program. Other ways to promote the course are holding informational sessions, presenting information at interagency conferences or community meetings, newsletters and social media. If there are other FDC certified leadership instructors in your community, we ask that you work together and coordinate efforts.

With continued emphasis on interagency collaboration in private and public grant funding, a creative option is to incorporate interagency FDC training as part of a grant proposal to demonstrate that all partners will be working together to achieve the collective goals of the proposed project. The credentialing fees and other expenses related to implementing the course can be included in the proposal budget.

Submitting FDC program forms

What to Submit	When to Submit It
Notice to Start form	At least two weeks prior to the first scheduled class, submitted to the FDC Program Manager.
	Upon receipt, the Program Manager will invoice for the Notice to Start fee (one per class).
Request for Portfolio Review form and final class list	After the last class session, submitted to the FDC Program Manager.
	Upon receipt, the Program Manager will invoice for the credentialing fee (per person).
Class portfolios	Within two weeks of the last class session, to the designated FDC Portfolio Reviewer.

Your role as facilitator

At one level, FDC classes provide "skills development" for family support professionals. However, many FDC instructors have found that over the course of training, participants experience complex levels of learning at deep and personal levels. This type of learning is sometimes referred to as "critical reflection" and is described as gathering information and comparing it with life experience in order to make sound decisions.

The underlying learning process of *Empowerment Skills for Leaders* is to help supervisors and leaders develop their critical reflection skills to use across the full spectrum of their work and personal life. Using critical reflection skills in everyday life situations involves the ability to:

1. Suspend the inclination to make decisions that draw on partial information, or rely on past experience, habits, or routines to solve new problems.

2. Recognize the ways that past experience and current knowledge affect the capacity to view a situation clearly and without bias.

3. Handle problems and difficulties flexibly and possess the willingness to reframe a situation or behavior when appropriate.

4. Step back from a situation to reflect on the process and look for discrepancies between actions and motivations.

5. Identify patterns of thought and actions within the organization that might be assets or areas in need of attention.

Teaching critical reflection skills is analogous to trying to "empower" someone—you can help them develop the skills to become more critically reflective, but only they can do the work. The goal of helping someone enhance their critical reflection skills is not to achieve some predetermined level of competency, but rather to move their skills further along the continuum toward a more conscious level of practice in daily life. For example, as a leader increases their skill in identifying the strengths of staff in their organization through activities developed in this course, it will hopefully lead to practicing these skills in the workplace and with interagency partners. Successfully practicing a skill in the workplace may, in turn, cause that skill to transfer to personal relationships. These new skills can create a revised pattern of thinking, feeling, and acting that eventually affects all one's relationships.

Facilitating the process of learning through experience, followed by critical reflection, helps participants develop new skills and competencies at their own pace and comfort level. The activities in *Empowerment Skills for Leaders* provide the opportunity for leaders to practice using strengths-based assessment, empowerment-based leadership, cultural humility, and supervising with "skill and heart." The role of the leadership facilitator is twofold: (1) to help leaders develop a broad range of leadership skills, and (2) to facilitate each leader's capacity for critical reflection.

The *Empowerment Skills for Leaders Instructor Manual* is a guide to help facilitators present the topics, skills, and concepts related to empowerment-based leadership. At the beginning of each chapter, there is a Schedule of Activities that includes the approximate time needed, and the accompanying power point slides and/or handouts. Keep in mind this is just an estimate. Generally, the larger the class size, the longer it will take to work through an activity. There are also suggestions for using Supplemental Resources that are optional but can be integrated to enhance the class sessions. Additional resources are listed on the FDC website, under Instructor Resources.

We ask that you facilitate a minimum of 30 hours of interactive classroom instruction. Most of the chapters have more than six hours of activities, which provides some flexibility in tailoring the activities to the needs and interests of the group, while still covering the main concepts and objectives. In addition, we encourage instructors to use the expertise of the group. For example, there might be a leader in the class with experience in dealing with workplace trauma or loss and grief. Other presenters with specialized expertise can also be invited to facilitate certain topics. An outside speaker can help create awareness of community and organizational resources that leaders may not be familiar with.

While the schedule and time frame for class sessions depends on what works best for the group, allowing enough time between classes for leaders to work on their portfolio is preferable. Meeting with their Peer Advisor can take place as part of a class session or at a convenient time outside of class but should not be counted as part of the 30 hours of required interactive classroom instruction.

Because *Empowerment Skills for Leaders* builds upon the strength-based concepts introduced in *Empowerment Skills for Workers*, there is a summary of what is covered in the workers course, along with a section on the adult learning process in Chapter 1 of the *Empowerment Skills for Leaders Handbook*. We felt this was important because not everyone who takes the leaders course is already familiar with the basic principles of family development. While this may be review material for some, we encourage instructors to provide some context on the background for both courses. In addition, we hope that leaders will support their staff to participate in the *Empowerment Skills for Workers* course in their local communities.

The following is a quote from an FDC leadership course participant:

> *This course has helped me to be more reflective in my interactions with others. It has encouraged me to reflect on how I interact with others and to reflect on what causes others to act/react the way that they do. This course has also given me the strength to be a better leader and manager, and to delegate more to staff. It also has encouraged me to be more organized in my work and to have more ownership over all aspects of the program.*

Table of Contents

CHAPTER 1
FAMILY DEVELOPMENT AND THE EMPOWERED WORKPLACE

Teaching materials

- Name tags or name place cards
- Computer/LCD projector/ smart board/power points
- Easel, easel paper, and markers
- Masking or cellophane tape
- Index cards (one for each participant)
- "Post-it" notes in two different colors
- Activity handouts, case studies and discussion questions
- Stand by Your Quotes (copied to post on walls)
- Core Principles of Family Development (copied to post on walls)
- A melodic bell or chime (to reconvene the group)
- Supplemental resources (optional)
- Refreshments (optional)

	Activities	Approximate Duration* (minutes)	Slides	Handouts/Materials
1	*Welcome, brief introductions, logistics, agenda*	15		
2	*Working Agreements*	10	S1 Working Agreements	
3	*Leadership Portfolio*	10	S2 The Leadership Portfolio S3 Peer Advisement	
4	*Chapter 1 learning objectives*	10	S4 Learning objectives for Chapter 1 S5 How Empowerment Skills for Leaders is different	
5	*Warmup activities: Who's Here Leadership Circle*	10		
	Stand by Your Quote	20		Stand by Your Quotes
6	*A bone-deep longing for freedom and self-respect*	30	S6 Bone-deep longing for freedom, self-respect, and hope S7 Bone-deep longing discussion questions	H1 Bone-deep longing discussion questions
7	*Recognizing the strengths and challenges of an empowered workplace*	30	S8 Characteristics of an empowered workplace	
8	*Definitions of empowerment*	30	S9 Definition of empowerment	H2 Definitions of empowerment survey
9	*Core Principles of Family Development*	30		Core principles of family development
10	*Shifting from a deficit to an empowerment approach*	30	S10 About Family S11 Shifting from a deficit to empowerment approach in the workplace S12 Deficit approach assumptions S13 Barriers to trust building with employees S14 The shared power approach	H3 Shifting from a deficit to empowerment approach in the workplace
11	*Effects of deficit and empowerment approaches in the workplace*	45		H4 Empowerment and deficit approaches in the workplace handout H5 Case studies H6 Worksheet

	Activities	Approximate Duration* (minutes)	Slides	Handouts/Materials
12	*Social forces affecting families, employees, organizations, and communities*	30	S15 Social forces that affect families, employees, organizations, and communities S16 Social forces discussion questions	
13	*Creating a Gracious Space*	30	S17 Core Elements of Gracious Space	
14	*Empowering leadership pitfalls and potential*	45		H7 Empowering leadership: Pitfalls and potentials case study H8 Questions
15	*Planning Independent Learning Projects*	30		Independent Learning Project
16	*Quick Feedback Form*	10		Quick Feedback Form

* Times are estimates and may vary according to group size and needs: approximately 6 hours per chapter, for a total of 30 hours.

Supplemental Resources

There are resources at the end of each chapter in the *Empowerment Skills for Leaders* Handbook. A suggestion would be to select one of the articles listed (or another of your choice) that you feel is relevant and of interest to the group and distribute copies for them to read (or refer them to a link online) before the next class session. At the beginning of the next class session, facilitate a brief discussion about the article and how it reinforces the concepts covered in the chapter.

Links to additional resources are on the FDC website, www.familydevelopmentcredential.org, under Instructor Resources.

Video

"Finding Strengths." Describes the core components of the family development approach and process presented by two families and their family development worker. Available on the FDC website, under Instructor Resources.

Websites

Clifton Strengths Assessment. "Strengths Finder."

Center for Ethical Leadership. "Gracious Space Self-Assessment."

http://www.ethicalleadership.org/uploads/2/6/2/6/26265761/1.3graciousspaceself-assessment.pdf.

Center for the Study of Social Policy. "Strengthening Families: Increasing Positive Outcomes for Children and Families." https://cssp.org/our-work/project/strengthening-families/.

Activities

1.   Welcome, brief introductions, logistics, agenda (15 min.)

- Welcome everyone to the session. Introduce yourself and briefly share your background related to leadership in the community and FDC.

- Distribute copies of the *Empowerment Skills for Leaders* handbook (if participants haven't already received it before this session).

- Ask participants to briefly introduce themselves: their name, agency, and position.

- Discuss the following logistics before starting the session:

  - Review the agenda including start, break, lunch, and end times.

  - Locations of restrooms

  - Host site policies regarding smoking, parking, etc.

  - Request to turn off or silence cell phones

  - Comfort check: encourage participants to request temperature changes and other adjustments as needed

2.   Working Agreements (10 min.)

Affirm that confidentiality is very important throughout this course. Explain that each member brings useful knowledge and experience to the group and that we can gain valuable insights from speaking openly with those with similar experiences.

Review the slide (S1) with the following list of suggested *Working Agreements* and ask for any additions:

- Respect confidentiality—what's said here, stays here.

- Listen.

- Say what you mean clearly and respectfully:

    - What happened?

    - What do you feel?

    - What do you want?

- Make encouraging comments: use "put ups".

- Ask questions.

- Take responsibility for the course going well.

- Humor is great!

- Silence phones.

- Others?

3.   The Leadership Portfolio (10 min.)

Review the course requirements as follows:

> To receive the National FDC Leadership Credential from the University of Connecticut, participants are required to attend a minimum of 90% of the class hours and complete a Leadership Portfolio.

> The Leadership Portfolio is developed throughout the course and provides an opportunity to apply the skills and concepts discussed in each chapter to your individual work environment.

Review slides S2 and S3.

It includes:

1. *One Independent Learning Project* for each of the five chapters that identifies, applies and reflects on a concept and/or competency that was discussed in the chapter.

2. *One Leadership Empowerment Plan* (and supporting documentation) that is reflective of the overall concepts and competencies in the curriculum.

3. *An Overall Reflection* that provides initial outcomes of the Leadership Empowerment Plan and describes how you are planning to implement empowerment-based leadership in the workplace.

4. *An Application* for the FDC Leadership Credential and Portfolio Checklist with signatures.

Continue:

> As your portfolio is developed, you will work with a Peer Advisor, sharing information about your projects and empowerment plan. Peer Advisors provide support and feedback to each other, including a written reflection for each of the Independent Learning Projects. The *Guide to Leadership Portfolio Development and Peer Advisement* gives more detail on the components of the portfolio and the role of Peer Advisors.

> Leadership Portfolios are submitted by the instructor to National FDC for review and approval before the leadership credential is issued.

> We'll have more discussion on Independent Learning Projects and the Peer Advisement process at the end of this session.

4.   Chapter 1 Learning Objectives (10 min.)

Review the *Learning Objectives for Chapter 1—Family Development and the Empowered Workplace* slide (S4):

- Learn the core concepts and competencies taught in *Empowerment Skills for Family Workers* and explore how they align with empowerment-based leadership.

- Recognize the characteristics of an empowered workplace.

- Understand the paradigm shift of "power over" to a "shared power" approach to leadership.

- Increase awareness of the difference between deficit-oriented practices and the family development approach in the workplace.

- Develop and offer services and programs consistent with the philosophy and best practices of family development.

- Through participation in community-based professional development, actualize the benefits of interagency and interdepartmental collaboration in achieving outcome-based goals.

Also review the *How Empowerment Skills for Leaders is different* slide (S5):

- Builds on specific skills and competencies leaders already have and that workers have learned through strength-based training.

- Provides an in-depth interactive and reflective program that encourages personal and organizational transformation.

- Developed for all levels of leadership in organizations from board members and executive directors to frontline supervisors.

- Identifies areas where empowerment-based change within the organization can begin to make meaningful differences in family support programs and agency-based outcomes.

- Promotes networking and collaboration among participants in a positive learning environment to support collective goals.

Briefly discuss these questions:

---

1. **What comes to mind when you think about the word "leadership"?**

2. **What are some of the benefits and challenges of implementing new strategies and concepts learned through professional development?**

---

5.   Warmup Activity: "Who's Here" Leadership Circle (10 min.)

There are two suggested warm-up activities for Chapter 1. Choose the one that best suits your group. The following activity works well for an interagency group or for a large organization where participants may not be very familiar with the various departments and their responsibilities.

Introduce this activity with a statement such as:

> This activity is a quick way to learn more about each other's organizations. Let's stand in a circle.

Invite the group to stand and form a circle.

> I'm going to read from a list of different characteristics found in organizations.
>
> If that characteristic applies to your organization or department, take a step into the circle. Look around to see who else is in the circle. Then, we'll all step out and I'll call out another characteristic. Participate at the level you feel comfortable, and you may choose not to step into the circle for any category. When I'm done, anyone is welcome to add characteristics that haven't been mentioned. Does anyone have a question before we start?

Once the group is standing in a circle, call out the following characteristics:

> Is your agency or organization...

- a not-for-profit agency?
- a county, state, or federal government agency?
- a for-profit business?
- another type of organization?

If people step in the circle, invite them to share a brief description. Then continue:

> Does your organization...

- serve only families with children?
- serve families that may not have children?
- help individuals and families across the life course?
- help families and individuals who are members of a specific cultural group? [If so, then invite them to briefly share.]
- provide assistance such as food, clothing, money, and other tangible items?
- provide home visiting, counseling, home health care, medical services, or educational training?
- provide services that are voluntary?
- provide services that are mandated?
- meet with families in their own homes or at places other than your office?
- operate all its services from a single location?
- operate with multiple centers?

- receive public or private grant funding?
- conduct fundraisers to support some of its programs?
- employ fewer than 10 people?
- employ between 10 and 40 people?
- employ more than 40 people?
- employ workers who were family members that the organization helped?
- require that workers have specialized training or degrees?
- have staff members who've worked there for more than 10 years?
- have supervisors or leaders who were former frontline workers?

Are there any other categories anyone else would like to ask about?

Conclude with:

This activity gives us an idea of what organizations are represented in our group and some things our agencies may have in common. Over the rest of the sessions, we'll have other opportunities to learn more about our organizations. Thanks for participating.

Warmup Activity: Stand by Your Quote* (20 min.)

This warm-up activity is an alternative to the Leadership Circle, particularly if the group is more familiar with each other's programs. It's a great way to get the group thinking about what leadership means to them.

Stand by Your Quote is a walk-about activity. In advance, print the quotes on the following page using type large enough to be easily read, and post each quote on the walls around the room. Invite participants to walk around reading the quotes and to stand by one that most resonates with their style of leadership in the workplace. Once everyone finds a quote, if there is more than one person there, ask them to discuss with each other why they chose that particular quote.

After a few minutes, process the activity with the entire group, reading each quote and asking the group to share why they selected and connected to its value in the workplace.

* Thanks to Angela Zimmerman, FDC instructor at Molloy College, Long Island, NY, for suggesting this warmup activity.

"A genuine leader is not a searcher for consensus but a molder of consensus."

~Dr. Martin Luther King, Jr.

"A leader is one who knows the way, goes the way, and shows the way."

~John C. Maxwell

"I've learned that people will forget what you said, people will forget what you did, but people will never forget how you made them feel."

~Maya Angelou

"The best leader is the one who has sense enough to pick good people to do what he wants done, and self-restraint to keep from meddling with them while they do it."

~Theodore Roosevelt

"Do not follow where the path may lead. Go instead where there is no path and leave a trail."

~Harold R. McAlindon

"The point of greatness is responsibility."

~Winston Churchill

"Leadership and learning are indispensable to each other."

~John F. Kennedy

"If your actions inspire others to dream more, learn more, do more, and become more, you are a leader."

~John Quincy Adams

"Never doubt that a small group of thoughtful, concerned citizens can change the world. Indeed, it is the only thing that ever has."

~Margaret Mead

"Be the change you want to see in the world."

~Mahatma Gandhi

6.   A bone-deep longing for freedom, self-respect, and hope (30 min.)

Introduce this activity with a statement such as:

> This quote from National FDC Director Claire Forest is the cornerstone of the Family Development Credential program. It expresses the values that leaders, workers, and family-serving organizations must all uphold to help all families, including our own families, to achieve healthy self-reliance and interdependence with our communities.

Read the *Bone-deep longing for freedom, self-respect, and hope* slide (S6) (or ask for volunteers to read).

> Let's separate into three groups to discuss ways that all people find healthy outlets to experience freedom, self-respect, and hope. Ask each group to record their ideas. Please choose one member to be the group's spokesperson to share ideas when we reconvene. Once you're together in three groups, I'll assign each group a question to discuss. You'll have five minutes to brainstorm ideas.

Ask the group to count off ("1, 2, 3") and convene in the corresponding group. Review the *Bone-deep longing for freedom, self-respect, and hope discussion questions* slide (S7), and assign each group a different question. In advance, make a copy of the *Bone-deep longing discussion questions* sheet (H1) on the next page. Separate the questions and give one question to each group.

After five minutes, reconvene the group and explain that each group had essentially the same question, but was asked to brainstorm ideas from the different perspectives of supervisors and leaders, staff members, and program participants. Ask each group's spokesperson to read their question and responses. Then, facilitate a brief discussion using the following questions:

1.   What similarities do you see between each group's responses?

2.   Why is it important that leaders and employees understand and promote the importance of self-reliance with program participants?

H1 Bone-deep longing discussion questions

Bone-deep longing for freedom, self-respect, and hope

Question 1

How do leaders and supervisors help staff members express their bone-deep longing for freedom, self-respect and hope?

Brainstorm a list of ways.

Bone-deep longing for freedom, self-respect, and hope

Question 2

How do family workers help families express their bone-deep longing for freedom, self-respect and hope? Brainstorm a list of ways.

Bone-deep longing for freedom, self-respect, and hope

Question 3

How does a person express their own bone-deep longing for freedom, self-respect and hope? Generate a list of ways.

----

7.   Recognizing the strengths and challenges of an empowered workplace (30 min.)

Introduce this activity with a statement such as:

> In Chapter 1, the analogy of Pandora's box introduces the benefits and challenges of supervising and leading an empowered workplace. Another analogy is to think of empowerment as a journey rather than a destination. Supervisors and leaders frequently respond to crises and the unexpected. Keeping your balance and focus on the organization's strengths when challenges arise can be difficult.

> Here are some characteristics and practices often found in an empowered workplace:

Read (or ask for volunteers to read) the *Characteristics of an empowered workplace* slide (S8). Distribute two Post-its of different colors to each participant.

> This activity will help you gain perspective on the strengths and challenges of an empowered workplace. On one Post-it, write the word "strength," then write an example of something positive happening in your organization. You can give more than one example if you want. On the other post it, write the word "challenge," then write an example of something that has interfered with achieving one or more of the characteristics of an empowered workplace.

Post two pieces of easel paper on the wall. Write "Strengths of an empowered workplace" on one, and "Challenges of an empowered workplace" on the other. Then continue:

> Once you've written a strength and challenge on your Post-its, please go to the corresponding easel paper and post the examples. You're welcome to talk about the strengths and challenges of your workplace with others at each station.

Review each list and then facilitate a brief discussion using these questions:

1.   What is the benefit of recognizing both strengths and challenges?

2.   How do organizational strengths and challenges affect each other?

3.   What strengths and challenges seem to be common areas for us?

8.   Definitions of Empowerment (30 min.)

Introduce this activity with a statement such as the following:

> The word empowerment is used in different contexts and can mean something different to workers and leaders, depending on individual circumstances. The meaning can also change over time.

Review the *Definition of Empowerment* slide (S9).

> This activity offers six definitions of empowerment based on various theoretical frameworks. While they all reflect aspects of empowerment, this exercise is intended to help you assess what empowerment means most to you right now and how that might differ from those you supervise.

Distribute the *Definitions of Empowerment Survey* handout (H2). Then continue:

> Take a few minutes to review the definitions and select the one that best describes what empowerment means to you right now.

After a few minutes, bring the group back together and discuss each definition. As they are comfortable sharing, ask why they chose a specific definition and what meaning it has for them.

Conclude with the following question:

> What are some ways that leaders can foster empowerment in staff members?

H2 Definitions of Empowerment Survey*

Write a checkmark next to the definition of empowerment that best describes what empowerment means to you right now.

Empowerment is…

_____ 1.   The outcome of a relationship where power is shared between partners to build an individual's capacity for and to set and reach their own goals. (*Partnership model of human services*, Darling 2000)

_____ 2.   The process of changing consciousness of individuals about the influence of power dynamics (especially surrounding domination and oppression) so they can learn to see reality in their own terms. (*Black feminist thought*, Hill Collins 2000)

_____ 3.   A learning process that is negotiated between a worker and program participant to become skilled and critical thinkers who are change agents and social critics. (*Critical thinking/Empowerment for social change*, Shor 1992)

_____ 4.   Development of personal efficacy (effectiveness) that enables people to take advantages of opportunities and to remove environmental constraints guarded by those whose interests are served by them. (*Self-efficacy*, Bandura 1997)

_____ 5.   An approach to a helping relationship focused on partnership, strengths, the linkage between the person and their environment, and that individuals have rights and responsibilities as a result of being members of a community. (*Ecological model of human development*, Bronfenbrenner 1979, Forest 2003; *Empowerment-based social work*, Lee 1994, Levy Simon 1994)

_____ 6.   A person's abilities to access resources, make decisions and solve problems, and acquire skills needed to interact effectively with others to secure resources. (*Family enablement*, Dunst et al. 1988)

* Thanks to Dr. Katie Palmer-House, who developed this survey as part of her doctoral thesis.

9.   The Core Principles of Family Development (30 min.)

In advance, copy and post the "Core Principles of Family Development" on walls around the room. Introduce this topic and activity with a statement such as:

> The Core Principles of Family Development are the "building blocks" of empowerment-based relationships—starting with identifying strengths in all individuals to creating conditions for systems to evaluate their own effectiveness. For this activity, you'll work in pairs and circulate the room reading and discussing each Core Principle. Each pair will have two sets of Post-it notes.
>
> - _____ colored notes indicate ways our agencies and community can take steps toward empowerment-based support for families.
>
> - _____ colored notes indicate actions needing change or to be reversed.
>
> Working in pairs, read over each principle and then post a (state the color) note next to each principle to describe one way to move toward that principle in your agency or community and/or move away from something that goes against it.
>
> For example, the first Core Principle is "All people, and all families, have strengths." If your agency or community wants to move further toward that principle, write a way it can be achieved using the (color) Post-it note. One response you might write on the Post-it might be "Include information about a family's strengths on the agency's intake form."
>
> If the principle describes something that agencies or the community are currently doing that goes against that principle that you want to move away from, use a (state the color) Post-it and give an example of something that could be done to change or reverse it.

Based on the size of the group, modify the number of principles each pair will review or allow enough time to do them all. Circulate and help pairs with brainstorming, as needed. Reconvene the group and ask for volunteers to read the principle and then, each of the Post-it notes. Conclude the activity with a brief discussion with the following question:

> Based on the number of notes in the two colors we've posted for each principle, is our group more inclined to believe that empowerment-based relationships occur through taking positive actions or changing negative actions in our agencies and community?

Conclude discussion with the idea that empowerment and family support require a balance of strengths-based, positive action and steps to correct and eliminate outdated and ineffective organizational and systems-level practices.

1. All people and all families have strengths.

2. The type and degree of support each family needs varies throughout the lifespan.

3. Most families are not dependent on long-term public support. Neither are they isolated. They maintain a healthy interdependence with extended family, friends, other people, spiritual organizations, cultural and community groups, schools and agencies, and the natural environment.

4. Diversity (race, ethnicity, gender, class, family form, religion, physical and mental ability, age, sexual orientation) is an important, valuable reality in our society. Family workers need to develop competence in working effectively with people who may be different from them or come from groups not often respected in our society.

5. The deficit model of family assistance, in which families must show inadequacy to receive services (and professionals decide what is best for them), is counterproductive to helping families move toward healthy self-reliance through a recognition of their strengths.

6. Changing from the deficit model to the family development approach requires a whole new way of thinking about social services, not simply more new programs. Individual workers cannot make this shift without corresponding policy changes at agency, state, and federal levels.

7. Families need coordinated services in which all the agencies they work with use a similar approach. Collaboration at the local, state, and federal levels is crucial to effective family development.

8. Families and family development workers are equally important partners in the empowerment process, with each contributing important knowledge. Workers learn as much as the families from the process.

9. Families must choose their own goals and methods of achieving them. Family development workers' roles include assisting families in setting reachable goals for their own self-reliance, providing access to services needed to reach these goals, and offering encouragement.

10. Services are provided in order for families to reach their goals and are not themselves a measure of success.

11.   In order for families to move out of dependency, helping systems must shift from a "power over" to a "power with" paradigm. Human service workers have power (which they may not recognize) because they participate in the distribution of valued resources. Workers can use that power to work with families rather than use power over them.

10. Shifting from a deficit to an empowerment approach in the workplace (30 min.)

Introduce this topic with a statement such as:

> The core concept of the family development approach is empowerment of families to achieve goals of healthy self-reliance and interdependence with their communities. In FDC, we use the term "family" very broadly.

Read or ask someone to read the *About Family* slide (S10).

> Family development is an "empowerment" model that emphasizes strengths, which is the opposite of the "deficit" model which emphasizes weaknesses. The deficit model is sometimes called the "provision of services" approach to family assistance. The empowerment model is also called the "family development" approach to family support. This diagram presents the differences between the deficit and empowerment models in the workplace.

Review the *Shifting from a deficit to empowerment approach in the workplace* slide (S11) and/or distribute as a handout (H3). This next slide summarizes the faulty assumptions of the deficit approach from a supervisor's perspective. Review the *Deficit approach assumptions* slide (S12). Then continue:

> Relationships built on trust are an Important aspect of the family development approach. Take a moment and think of someone you trust and someone you don't … and consider why?

Pause for a few moments. Then continue:

> Here are some barriers to trust building.

Review the *Barriers to trust building with employees* slides (S13). Ask If there are any other barriers they want to add. Then continue:

> In contrast, these are characteristics of the "shared power" or "power with" approach which promote trust building.

Review *The shared power approach* slide (S14).

> In the *Empowerment Skills for Workers* course, workers learn that their role is to help families empower themselves in achieving their goals of healthy self-reliance. Workers do this by helping identify their strengths, helping them develop and plan goals, and offering services and support when needed. Workers learn that the paradigm shift from the deficit to empowerment approach often requires changes at program, organizational, and family support systems levels. It is important that managers and supervisors support their staff in making this paradigm shift. Empowerment-based leadership is also foundational to this approach.

Facilitate a brief discussion using the following questions:

1. **What day-to-day changes might occur in organizations that adopt an empowerment or family development approach with staff members?**

2. **How does the shift from a deficit to empowerment model affect the relationships between supervisors and leaders, and staff members?**

Write the group's ideas on easel paper. Conclude with the idea that upcoming sessions will provide practical information to help supervisors and leaders make the shift toward empowerment-based relationships in their organization.

H3 Shifting from a deficit to an empowerment approach in the workplace

Deficit approach to family support

- Families who need support must have something wrong with them.
- Professionals know what's best for families.
- Using incentives and sanctions builds healthy self-reliance.
- Providing services is the goal of human service agencies.

"Power over" approach in the workplace

- The supervisor knows all relevant information about situations that involve workers and families.
- Supervisors and leaders know what's best for staff and families.
- Unless monitored closely, staff members will be lazy and dishonest.
- Staff will follow up on whatever is recommended.

Empowerment approach to family development

- The goal of restoring dignity to families cannot be accomplished by adding another program to existing programs.
- Relationships built on "shared "power" help families become self-reliant.
- Family development is based on the strengths and needs of families.

"Power with" approach in the workplace

- Staff members know their strengths and challenges best.
- Staff members are most successful in accomplishing plans they create in consultation with their supervisor, not plans supervisors make for them.
- Leaders see staff members as assisting them in recognizing their strengths and challenges.
- Leaders support staff members in accomplishing mutually agreed-upon goals.

11. Effects of empowerment and deficit approaches in the workplace (45 min.)

Introduce this activity with an opening statement such as:

> In most circumstances, supervisors and leaders have the choice to make decisions based on an empowerment ("shared power") or a deficit ("power over") approach. Even if the outcome is the same using either approach, exerting "power over" generally results in a "domino" effect of negative attitudes and responses in relationships. Workers respond in much the same way that families would when dealing with a "power over" approach. Let's review some of the differences in the way a supervisor and worker might feel, think, and act based on using an empowerment or deficit approach in their relationship.

Review (or ask for volunteers to read) the *Empowerment and deficit approaches in the workplace* handout (H4) and distribute the *Empowerment and deficit approaches in the workplace case studies* handout (H5).

> We're going to read four case situations in which a leader must decide how to approach a situation where deficit or empowerment-based leadership can be used. After we read them, choose one situation that interests you (or assign them randomly). One corner of the room will be designated for each case situation. Each group will work together for about 10 minutes to develop how this situation might unfold from a "shared power" and "power over" approach. Please designate a spokesperson to present the group's ideas.

Designate four areas of the room for people to meet and give each group a copy of the *Empowerment and deficit approaches in the workplace* worksheet (H6).

After 10–15 minutes, ask each group's spokesperson to read their case situation and worksheet responses. Conclude the activity with a brief discussion using these questions:

1. What can a supervisor and leader do to change a relationship if it's already been long-established in a deficit ("power over") approach?

2. Why might staff members be resistant to changing a relationship with their supervisor if it has been based on a "power over" approach?

H4 Empowerment and deficit approaches in the workplace

Concept	Shared Power (Empowerment)	Power Over (Deficit)
Worker's Frame of Reference	"I am responsible for my goals and future."	"The organization owes it to me."
Worker–Supervisor Relationship	Mutual respect for one another's talents and roles Worker and Supervisor develop and set goals together	Supervisor decides what a worker needs. Supervisor assumes a worker is not competent so must be constantly monitored.
Supervisor's Frame of Reference	What is strong with this worker (and how can I help build on it)?	What is wrong with this worker? How can I make them fix it)?
Supervisor's Focus	Focus on supporting ongoing healthy worker development	Focus on current crisis
Power Dynamic	"Power with" or "shared power"	Power "over"
Supervisor's View of Diversity	Individual differences and staff diversity are valuable.	Workers should "fit in."

H5 Empowerment and Deficit Approaches in the Workplace
Case Studies

Situation 1

Funding for a well-established family support program in your organization has been unexpectedly cut because of a change in priorities. Loss of funding for this program will result in the need to lay off some newly hired workers who have brought much needed creativity and cultural diversity to your organization. You need to decide how best to approach the situation while keeping staff morale and productivity stable during the transition.

Situation 2

Your organization is in the process of restructuring departments and senior management responsibilities. You have been reassigned as the Director of a new department that you know very little about after the past Director left the position and the organization without explanation. You need to consider how you want to begin or re-establish relationships with supervisors and workers within your organization in this new capacity.

Situation 3

You are a supervisor, who is told by your supervisor that due to unanticipated expenditures that were not budgeted for, there will not be the annual cost-of-living salary increase for staff. The program you supervise, despite having some changes in staffing through the year, has a strong team ethic and consistently met or exceeded program outcomes. Employees are upset and want to know why this happened and when the salary increases will be given.

Situation 4

You are the Executive Director of an organization required by funding sources to provide outcome-based measures and verification to demonstrate that program participants are meeting these outcomes. While time consuming, the current forms used do not provide adequate information for reporting purposes. You need to revise the forms and inform the staff they will be responsible for ensuring that program outcomes are met.

H6 Worksheet: Empowerment and Deficit Approaches in the Workplace

Choose one of the case studies and develop responses for each category that reflects the differences between using an empowerment (shared power) and deficit (power over) approach.

Concept	Shared Power (Empowerment)	Power Over (Deficit)
Worker's Frame of Reference		
Worker–Supervisor Relationship		
Supervisor's Frame of Reference		
Supervisor's Focus		
Power Dynamic		
Supervisor's View of Diversity		

12. Social forces affecting families, employees, organizations, and communities (30 min.)

Introduce this topic and activity with a statement such as:

> Powerful social forces affect communities and the way that organizations can provide services and support. Here is a partial list of some of those forces:

Review the *Social forces that affect families, employees, organizations, and communities* slide (S15):

> Working with a partner, choose one of the social forces from the list or a different one that is not on the list and discuss how that social force affects:
>
> - The well-being of communities
> - Quality of life for families/program participants
> - Quality of life for employees of your organization
> - The work of your organization

Put up the *Social forces discussion questions* slide (S16). After about 10 minutes, ask for volunteers to share their ideas about the impact of the social forces they discussed. Conclude with discussion on the following question:

> What can supervisors and leaders do to channel social forces in ways that benefit our employees and organizations?

13. Creating a Gracious Space (30 min.)

Introduce the activity with a statement such as:

> As we think about creating an "empowered" workplace, it is not only about what we do, but also about the environment we create. "Gracious Space" is a concept and body of work developed by the Center for Ethical Leadership to describe a powerful approach to workplace inclusion. It is defined as "a spirit and setting where we invite the stranger and learn in public". Gracious Space creates an environment for being intentional, welcoming diverse opinions, listening deeply and learning together.

Review the *Core Elements of Gracious Space* slide (S17). Then, ask the group to consider the following question individually for a few minutes:

> Think of a time you experienced Gracious Space—whatever that means to you. What was the setting? What did you experience?

After a few minutes, have the group break into pairs and share their experiences with each other for about five minutes.

Convene the large group and ask them to share some general characteristics of the Gracious Space they experienced. Write their responses on easel paper.

Conclude by saying:

> Your stories and descriptions indicate you already know quite a bit about Gracious Space. The Center for Ethical Leadership has an excellent toolkit with exercises to assist leaders in implementing Gracious Space in the workplace.

> In this space, we can work better across boundaries, share diverse perspectives, work through conflict, discover transformative solutions and carry out innovations for change.

14.   Empowering leadership: Pitfalls and potential (45 min.)

Introduce this activity with a statement such as:

> Perhaps the most significant challenge in leading an empowered workplace is to take time to step back and reflect on how your experiences present opportunities for personal and professional growth.

> Let's read this passage from one leader's experience working in an empowered workplace. Then, each of three groups will discuss specific questions, each group with a different focus and task.

Read (or ask for volunteers to read) the *Empowering leadership: pitfalls and potential case study* handout (H7).

> Let's separate into three groups, and each group will have a different focus for discussion. One group will be called: "Support." This group will identify this leader's strengths and share similar experiences they might have had in this type of situation. The second group is called "Challenge." This group will explore ways to help this leader critically reflect on how they got to this point, and what to do next. The third group is called "Reflection." This group will explore this leader's underlying beliefs and values and how they might influence future actions.

Designate three areas of the room for small group discussions related to the three areas of discussion: "Support," "Challenge," and "Reflection." Ask participants to go to the corresponding area of discussion (Support, Challenge or Reflection) that interests them. Pass out the corresponding questions from the *Empowering leadership case study questions* sheet (H8). Provide each group with easel paper and marker and ask them to designate a spokesperson to present responses of questions to the entire group.

After 10 minutes, ask the groups to present their responses for each area. Allow for comments from participants, but don't bring up new questions. Facilitate a summarizing discussion using the following question.

> Based on our discussion, what suggestions would you give to a leader who wants to develop a more empowered workplace?

H7 Empowering leadership: Pitfalls and potential case study

"The shift to developing programs focused on outcomes and accountability has really changed things for our agency. In many ways we were ready, but in some areas, we were not.

In the past, we measured our success as an organization based on meeting the goals projected in a grant proposal, or the percentage increase in the number of services we provided this year compared with last year. We've realized now that a goal is not always an outcome and focusing on outcomes is where we need to be.

At the organizational level, for example, a goal may be helping my staff members get the training they need to perform their jobs well. But achieving the outcome of an empowered workplace means going the next step. Leaders need to look beyond staff training as a single remedy to move their agency to empowerment-based family support. In an outcome-based family support environment, leaders are the ones responsible to make things happen; they should be willing to make changes and take actions so staff members can use their skills with families, co-workers, and collaborators effectively.

Sticking with a "power with" approach seems easiest when things are going well. But in tough times or during a crisis, leaders need to act fast and make the right decision the first time. That's especially difficult nowadays because agencies and systems are much more interconnected. If a collaborator has difficulties, or our community is faced with a problem- even a national situation can affect us in ways that put us into crisis mode…

Our organization makes a lasting difference in the lives of our families and serves an important need in the community. With so much to think about and look out for in making sure everything runs smoothly, it's a challenge sometimes for me to see where my own contribution comes in to making that difference."

H8 Empowering leadership case study questions for small-group discussion

Copy and separate each set of questions for small group discussion.

Questions for small group discussion focused on offering *Support*:

1. What are the personal and professional strengths this leader brings to this situation?

2. When a leader facilitates a major change in their organization, what other strengths and supports are helpful to have?

3. Have you, or anyone you've known, ever experienced a major organizational change? If so, what strengths came out in the process?

Questions for small-group discussion focused on the handling the *Challenge*:

1. What has this leader learned about themselves through this experience so far?

2. How did facilitating a major change in the organization affect this leader in a way that they didn't expect?

3. What else could a leader do to prepare for facilitating a major change in their organization?

Questions for discussion focused on using *Reflection*:

1. What are some personal beliefs and values this leader has about empowerment?

2. How do those beliefs and values support or interfere with this leader's understanding about facilitating major change in the organization?

3. What is the next thing you'd recommend this leader do to guide the organization through this change?

15. Planning Independent Learning Projects (30 min.)

Explain that the purpose of Independent Learning Projects is to help supervisors and leaders relate their knowledge and understanding of the curriculum to benefit and support their professional practice. Each chapter offers a few ideas for different independent learning projects; *however, participants are strongly encouraged to create their own project that is meaningful and relevant to their workplace.*

For each learning project, participants are asked to work with another participant in the group who will serve as a "peer advisor" for that chapter. The role of the peer advisor is to help them develop a manageable task and time frame for the project, and to provide support and encouragement in achieving the outcome. Participants are encouraged to collaborate with a different peer advisor for each chapter.

The peer advisor is asked to work *with* their partner to develop the plan. After the project is completed, the leader and peer advisor meet again to discuss how the plan went. After that discussion, the peer advisor is asked to provide a brief written strengths-based reflection on the Independent Learning Project Plan sheet and sign the form. The reflection should be written to the person completing the plan (not to the portfolio reviewer) describing that person's strengths and insights related to empowerment-based leadership skills.

Invite them to spend a few minutes thinking about creating their own project that demonstrates an aspect of the curriculum they have learned in the first chapter.

After identifying a project or idea, ask them to find a partner to serve as their peer advisor for this chapter (and they will also be their partner's peer advisor for this chapter). Ask them to spend time with their peer advisor developing and preparing a plan for an Independent Learning Project. Then ask them to spend time developing their own plan with their partner providing support as a peer advisor. Encourage them to choose a manageable task and project time frame and to provide support to each other between sessions, scheduling their discussion at mutually convenient times.

Empowerment Skills for Leaders
Independent Learning Project

Name: _____   Chapter: _____

Description of independent learning project: (including date, participants, and setting)

_____

_____

_____

Reflection on this experience: (use this space or attach other sheets)

_____

_____

_____

_____

_____

_____

_____

_____

Reviewed with Peer Advisor: _____   _____
                                      Peer Advisor's signature   Date

Peer Advisor's Reflection

_____

_____

_____

Leader's Signature/Date   _Leadership Facilitator's Signature/Date_

16. Quick Feedback form (10 min.)

Thank people for their time and participation in coming to the session. In advance, make enough copies of the feedback form and distribute to participants at the end of the day. Remind them that the feedback is extremely important and that you'll summarize the overall comments at the next session.

Empowerment Skills for Leaders

Chapter 1: Family Development and the Empowered Workplace

Quick Feedback Form

When during the session did you feel most engaged?

When during the session did you feel least engaged?

What would make your experience in this course better?

Thanks for your feedback!

Chapter 1 PowerPoint slides

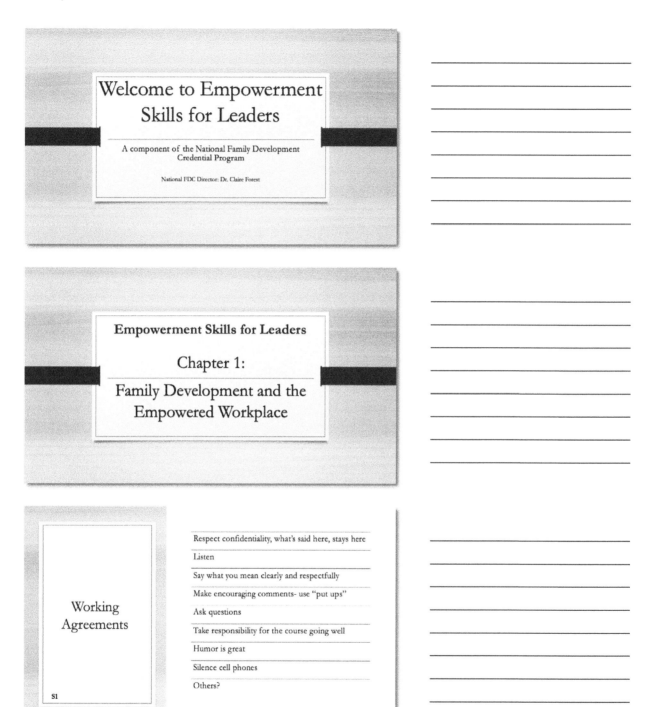

The Leadership Portfolio

* *One* **Independent Learning Project** *for each of the five chapters* that applies and reflects on a concept and/or competency discussed in the chapter.

* *One* **Leadership Empowerment Plan** that identifies a short-term goal and outlines steps to achieve it.

* An **Overall Reflection** summarizing what you've learned and how you will continue to implement the skills and concepts of empowerment-based leadership.

* An **Application for the FDC Leadership Credential and Portfolio Checklist** with signatures.

S2

Peer Advisement

Peer Advisors provide support and feedback to each other, including a written reflection for each of the Independent Learning Projects and follow-up with the Leadership Empowerment Plan.

S3

Chapter 1: Learning Objectives

* Learn the core concepts and competencies taught in *Empowerment Skills for Family Workers* and explore how they align with empowerment-based leadership.

* Recognize the characteristics of an empowered workplace.

* Understand the paradigm shift of "power over" to a "shared power" approach to leadership.

* Increase awareness of the difference between deficit-oriented practices and the family development approach.

S4

Learning Objectives (continued)

* Develop and offer services and programs consistent with the philosophy and best practices of family development.

* Through participation in community-based professional development, actualize the benefits of interagency and interdepartmental collaboration in achieving outcome-based goals.

S4

How is *Empowerment Skills for Leaders* unique?

* Builds on specific skills and competencies you already have

* Provides an interactive and reflective experience that encourages personal and organizational transformation

* Developed for all levels of leadership in organizations

* Helps identify where empowerment-based change within the organization can make meaningful differences in programs and outcomes

* Promotes networking and collaboration among participants in a positive learning environment

S5

A bone-deep longing...

Within each person *lies a bone-deep longing for freedom, self-respect, hope, and the chance to make an important contribution to one's family, community, and the world.*

Without healthy outlets for this powerful, natural longing, the desire for freedom turns into lawlessness, and the need for self-respect is expressed in aggression and violence.

Without avenues to make important contributions to family, community, and the world, hopelessness translates into dependency, depression, violence, substance abuse and other forms of self-abuse.

No government program can help families become self-reliant, contributing members of their communities unless it is built on a recognition of the power of this bone-deep longing for freedom, self-respect, hope, and the chance to make an important contribution.   Claire Forest

S6

Bone-deep longing discussion questions

1) How can leaders and supervisors help staff members express their bone-deep longing for freedom, self-respect and hope?

2) How can staff members help program participants express their bone-deep longing for freedom, self-respect and hope?

3) How does an individual express their own bone-deep longing for freedom, self-respect and hope?

S7

Characteristics of an empowered workplace

* Creative and talented employees who represent diverse cultures and experiences across the lifespan.

* Employees who understand their role and how their individual efforts contribute to the agency and its overall mission.

* Employees and supervisors who are committed to creating relationships based on mutual respect, recognizing individual strengths, and working on common goals.

S8

Characteristics of an empowered workplace (continued)

* Employees who feel respected, listened to, and welcomed.

* Leaders who build and strengthen cooperative relationships within the agency and the community to share resources and address gaps in service.

* Leaders who understand that each person has a bone-deep longing for freedom, safety, self-respect, hope, and the chance to make important contributions to one's family, community and the world.

S8

Definition of empowerment

The process of becoming stronger and more confident, especially in controlling one's life and claiming one's rights.

It is a dynamic process through which employees set and reach their own goals. **No one can "empower" someone else.**

S9

About "Family"

Families define themselves. Families are big, small, extended, nuclear, multi-generational, with one parent, two parents, and grandparents. We live under one roof or many. A family can be as temporary as a few weeks, as permanent as forever. We become part of a family by birth, adoption, marriage, or from a desire for mutual support. As family members, we nurture, protect and influence each other. Families are dynamic and cultures into themselves, with different values and unique ways of realizing dreams. Together, our families become the source of our rich cultural heritage and spiritual diversity. Each family has strengths and qualities that flow from individual members and from the family as a unit. Our families create neighborhoods, communities, states and nations...

Developed and adopted by the New Mexico Legislative Young Children's Continuum and the New Mexico Coalition for Children.

S10

Shifting from a deficit to an empowerment approach in the workplace

S11

An understanding of power is important for both supervisors and staff members.

Power, and its use or abuse influences whether staff members stay dependent or become self-reliant and whether they are effective or ineffective.

Understanding this power dynamic helps supervisors support staff in building mutually respectful relationships and effective partnerships with program participants.

Deficit approach assumptions

* Supervisors know all the relevant information about situations that involve employees
* Supervisors and leaders know what's best for staff
* Unless closely monitored, staff members will not be productive
* Staff members will follow up on whatever is recommended

S12

Barriers to trust-building with employees

* Lack of respect between leaders, supervisors and staff
* Learning to play roles that perpetuate the power imbalance
* Misinformation about others that leads to stereotypes, prejudice, and discrimination
* Staff who feel embarrassed and defensive when they need to seek help
* Employee attitudes and workplace limitations

S13

Barriers to trust-building (continued)

Relationships built on the "power over" approach almost never help people become self-reliant.

They may lead to meeting some short-term goals of the agency, but they do not create the conditions that lead to long term self-reliance for employees.

S13

The "shared power" approach

* Employees know their strengths and challenges best
* Staff are most successful in accomplishing plans they create in consultation with their supervisor, not plans that are made for them
* Leaders see their role with staff as assisting them in recognizing their strengths and challenges
* Leaders support staff in accomplishing mutually agreed upon goals

S14

Social forces affecting families, employees, organizations and communities

* Widening gap between the "haves" and "have nots"
* Changing structure, role and function of families
* Cultural impact of new waves of immigration and resettlement
* Violence, in families, communities and the workplace
* Challenge of racial and gender diversity and leadership

* People living longer
* Economic globalization
* Climate change
* Technology and social media
* Vanishing privacy
* Opioid epidemic
* COVID-19 pandemic of 2020

S15

Social forces discussion questions

Choose one social force and discuss how it affects:

1) The well-being of communities
2) The work of our organizations
3) The quality of life for employees and families

What can supervisors and leaders do to channel social forces in ways that benefit employees, families and communities?

S16

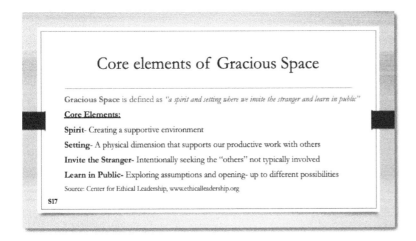

CHAPTER 2
TRANSFORMING YOUR WORKPLACE THROUGH EMPOWERMENT-BASED LEADERSHIP

Teaching materials

- Computer/LCD projector/smart board/PowerPoint slides

- Easel, easel paper, and markers

- Masking or cellophane tape

- Activity handouts and materials

- A melodic bell or chime (to reconvene the group)

- Supplemental Resources (optional)

- Refreshments (optional)

	Activities	Approximate Duration (minutes)	Slides	Handouts/Materials
1	*Agenda and Ch. 1 Feedback Summary*	10		
2	*Ch. 2 Learning Objectives*	5	S1 Chapter 2: Learning objectives	
3	*Are you ready? Icebreaker*	20		H1 Are you ready? Icebreaker key and mystery words
4	*Making the paradigm shift to empowerment-based leadership*	40	S2 Paradigm shift graphic S3 Two paradigm shifts of empowerment-based leadership	H2 Effects of the paradigm shift from deficit to empowerment approach
5	*FDC Core Principles adapted for supervisors and leaders*	30	S4 FDC Core Principles adapted for supervisors and leaders	H3 FDC Supervisory Core Principles adapted for supervisors and leaders
6	*Models of effective supervision*	30–45	S5 Transactional models of supervision S6 Interactional models of supervision S7 What's the difference? S8 Four approaches of developmental supervision S9 Reflective leadership skills	
7	*Servant and connective leadership*	30	S10 Essentials of effective leadership S11 Qualities of servant leadership S12 Qualities of connective leadership	
8	*What's your leadership style?*	30–60		H4 Recognizing your leadership styles H5 Leadership Compass approaches to work
9	*Recognizing the natural assets of staff members*	40	S13 "What's going right?" focus group quote S14 Recognizing natural assets of employees	H6 Helping staff build on their strengths
10	*Aligning your leadership vision with organizational vision*	30	S15 Aligning your vision with the mission of the organization	H7 Worksheet: Aligning your vision with the mission of the organization

Activities	Approximate Duration (minutes)	Slides	Handouts/Materials
11 *Workplace Empowerment Plan*	60		H8 Workplace Empowerment Plan role play H9 Short-term goals for workplace empowerment H10 Workplace Empowerment Plan
12 *Assessing the level of empowerment in your workplace*	30	S16 Definition of "empowerment" in family development S17 Conflicts between competing beliefs S18 Ways workers try to reconcile conflict between competing beliefs	H11 Situations to assess the level of empowerment in your workplace
13 *Building your agency's capacity for transformation*	20	S19 Three types of change in organizations S20 Guidelines for building your agency's capacity for transformation	
14 *"Talking the talk" and "walking the walk"*	30	S21 Principles of empowerment-based assessment S22 Guidelines for developing empowerment-based assessment	
15 *Planning Independent Learning Projects*	30		
16 *Quick Feedback Form*	10		Quick Feedback Form

Supplemental Resources

There are resources at the end of each chapter in the *Empowerment Skills for Leaders* Handbook. A suggestion would be to select one of the articles listed (or another of your choice) that you feel is relevant and of interest to the group and distribute copies for them to read (or refer them to a link online) before the next class session. At the beginning of the next class session, facilitate a brief discussion about the article and how it reinforces the concepts covered in the chapter.

Links to additional resources are on the FDC website, www.familydevelopmentcredential.org, under Instructor Resources.

Website

Be the Change Consulting. "Leadership Compass Self-Assessment." 2010. https://www.bethechangeconsulting.com/sites/default/files/worksheets/Leadership-compass-self-assessment.pdf.

Activities

1.   Agenda and Chapter 1 Feedback Summary (10 min.)

Welcome everyone back and thank them for coming.

Provide a short summary of feedback from the last session. Highlight positive comments and if needed, discuss any feedback that you think the group needs to process or give you further information on.

2.   Chapter 2 Learning Objectives (5 min.)

Read (or ask volunteers to read) the *Learning Objectives for Chapter 2: Transforming Your Workplace through Empowerment-Based Leadership* slide (S1):

- Learn how the family development approach aligns with effective models of supervision.

- Reflect on your personal leadership style and how it may vary with different staff members.

- Recognize the natural assets of staff members and strengths of the organization.

- Align your leadership vision with the mission of your organization.

- Assess the level of empowerment in your workplace.

- Understand the different types of organizational change and ways to build your agency's capacity for transformation.

- Identify key components of family-focused and outcome-based program assessment and compare to what your agency is currently using.

- Strengthen interagency collaborations.

- Learn about and connect with state and national family support initiatives.

3.   Are you ready? Warmup Activity (20 min.)

In advance, copy and post the five Mystery Word sheets around the room.

Introduce this activity with a statement such as:

> In Chapter 2, the book describes the analogy of transforming your organization through empowerment-based leadership to preparing for a trip. Just as there are many steps in planning a trip, using the skills of empowerment-based leadership will help you and your organization make the journey of organizational transformation. "Are you ready to begin?"
>
> This activity requires that you and a partner complete a task together. There are five pieces of paper posted on the walls around the room. On each sheet, there are short lines with different shapes on them. The short lines are spaces for letters of the alphabet representing words that are important concepts in this chapter. On some lines, there are shapes. Each team will receive a slip of paper with letters of the alphabet that correspond to each shape as a clue to figure out the word.
>
> You and your partner are asked to figure out the "mystery" word on all five sheets. You can talk with each other, but don't talk with other pairs or give away the answers. You can start at any sheet you'd like. You'll have about five minutes to do this. Are there questions? Now, choose a partner; one of you can come get a "clue" key (H1) and then begin.

The words are:

- Mystery Word 1—*Paradigm*

- Mystery Word 2—*Empowerment*

- Mystery Word 3—*Transformation*

- Mystery Word 4—*Assessment*

- Mystery Word 5—*Shared Power*

After about five minutes, congratulate the group and ask partners to sit together. Ask the pairs to quickly brainstorm a list of all the things they did to complete the task. Encourage them to think about what they did from the time the directions were given until the task was finished.

Facilitate a brief discussion using these questions:

1. Thoughtful preparation makes a task more manageable to achieve. What were some things you and your partner did to "get ready" to complete this task?

2. If you're preparing to transform your organization using empowerment-based leadership, what do you need to do to "get ready?"

H1 Are You Ready? Clue Key

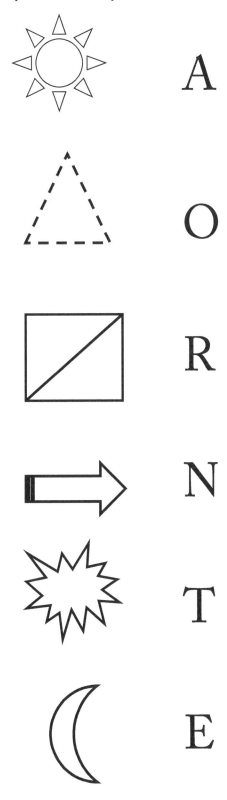

Mystery Word 1

Mystery Word 2

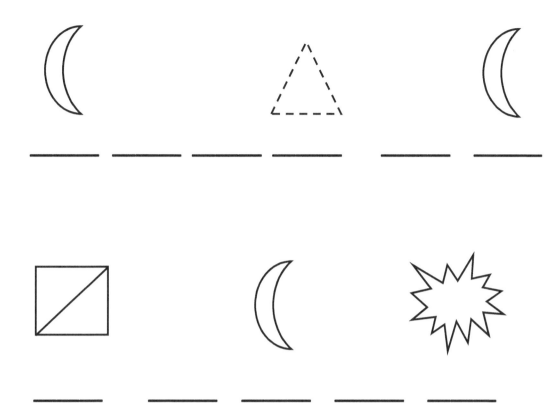

Mystery Word 3

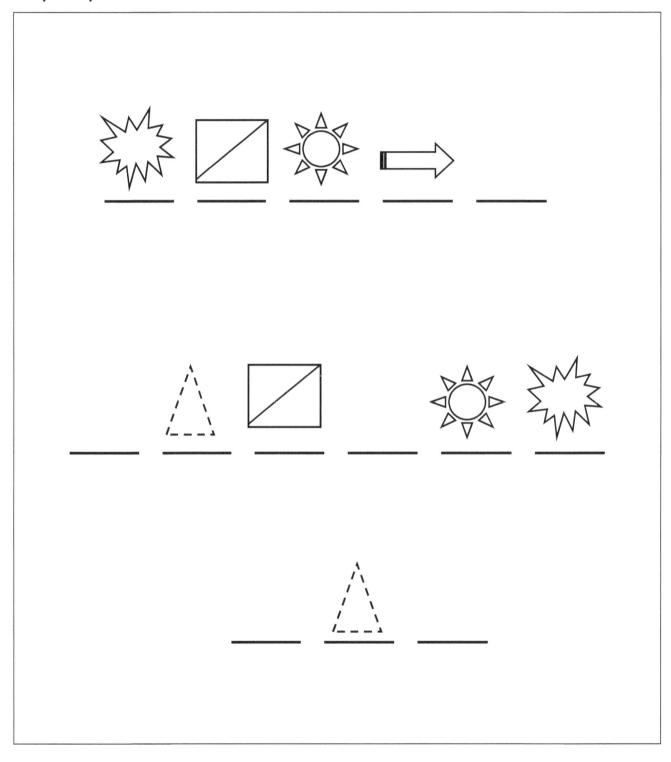

Mystery Word 4

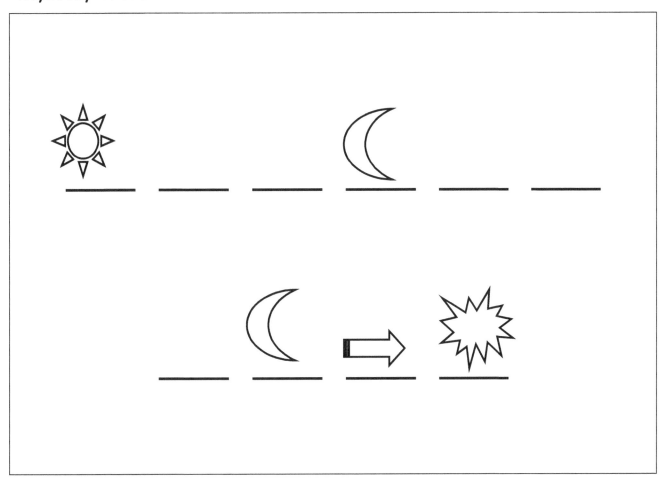

Mystery Word 5

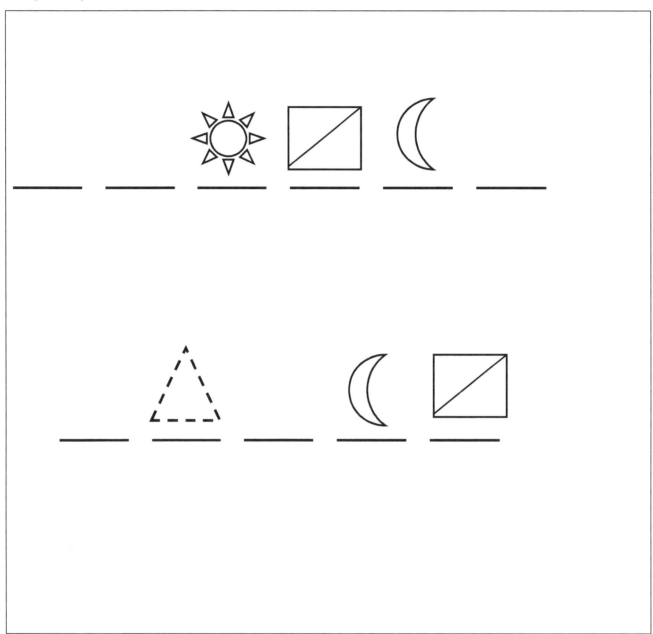

4.   Making the paradigm shift to empowerment-based leadership (40 min.)

Introduce this topic with a statement such as:

> A paradigm is a pattern of thinking and acting. Paradigms are like habits we've developed over time. Changing a habit that you've had for a long time or trying to develop a new one can be a challenge. This activity will give you a sense of how a pattern can be ingrained in everyday behavior, and how it might feel to try and change it.

Ask the group to use a blank sheet of paper (provide some if needed) and fold it horizontally in half to make top and bottom portions. Put up the *Paradigm shift graphic* slide (S2). Ask participants to draw the graphic on one half of the sheet. Mention that no one will be asked to show his or her drawing. Reassure those who say they can't draw that the activity is *not* related to artistic ability.

After about a minute, advise people that they don't need to finish the drawing and there is another step in this activity. Ask participants to draw the graphic again on the other half of the sheet with their "non-dominant" hand. After about two minutes, ask people to finish and lead a brief discussion using these questions:

---

1. How did it feel to copy the graphic with your dominant hand?

2. How did it feel to copy the graphic with your non-dominant hand?

3. Have you ever changed a longtime habit?

4. What are some things you had to do, or stop doing, to change the habit?

Expect that some participants will report finding the task easy, fun, frustrating, or embarrassing. If you are comfortable, share your own experience of doing the activity or relate an experience you've had in changing a longtime habit. Encourage participants to consider how their "non-dominant" drawing might improve given more time or practice.

Explain that this activity provides a sense of how it might feel to make a shift in a pattern of thinking or acting on a *personal* level. Today's leaders need encouragement and support to make paradigm shifts on a *public* level. Changing an organization's engrained habits of thinking and acting can affect everyone in both personal and professional ways.

Review the *Two paradigm shifts of empowerment-based leadership* slide (S3). Facilitate a discussion using these questions:

---

1. What do you think might happen if supervisors and leaders made paradigm shifts in these areas?

2. How would families be affected if supervisors and leaders made paradigm shifts from "power over" to "shared power" in their agencies?

If you sense group anxiety through either a lack of response to these questions, or by negative statements about the impact of these paradigm shifts on the organization, reassure participants that supervisors and leaders have a critical role, but not sole responsibility, for making these paradigm shifts.

Explain that the vision to empower families, workers, organizations, and collaborations may *begin* with them, but that it is interwoven with the efforts of families, workers, collaborators, policy makers and many others.

Review the *Effects of the paradigm shift from deficit to empowerment at the family service system level* handout (H2) (this diagram is also presented in *Empowerment Skills for Leaders*, Chapter 1).

In presenting the second paradigm shift to "empowering, compassionate support," remind participants that this paradigm shift doesn't require leaders to do *more*, but rather to do things differently—to move away from leadership that focuses on "power over" or "providing services" to staff members, and toward leadership that focuses on "shared power" and "providing support."

If you can, share information about the progress of local FDC programs and collaborations that are using the principles and practices of the *Empowerment Skills for Family Workers* curriculum in their organizations and communities. Refer to the creation and accomplishments of local and state coalitions that are working toward the vision of shared power with families. Mention that those efforts are becoming more widely embraced across a wide variety of professions that provide family-focused support.

H2 Effects of the paradigm shift from deficit to empowerment at the family service system level

START HERE and read clockwise Leaders of family-serving agencies support worker and allocate adequate resources for family-focused programs and services.

Workers in family-serving agencies help families reclaim their ability to dream and to create, plan, and achieve goals of healthy self-reliance.

Families become increasingly more self-reliant, contributing members of their communities.

National and local family support associations raise awareness about family support practice and strengthen local advocacy efforts.

The individual experiences her/his bone-deep longing for freedom, self-respect, hope, and the chance to make an important contribution to her/his family, community, and the world.

National and state elected officials enact legislation that promotes family-centered support to families across the lifespan.

Policymakers develop procedures and guidelines that demonstrate and strengthen the commitment to involve families in the process of family development.

Funding sources support programs that demonstrate how innovative programs and inter-agency collaboration help famlies achieve healthy interdependence with their communities.

Family-serving agencies work cooperatively and collaboratively in their communities to achieve family-focused outcomes and bridge gaps in services.

5.   The FDC Core Principles adapted for supervisors and leaders (30 min.)

In advance, make copies of the FDC Core Principles adapted for supervisors and leaders and post them on walls around the room.

Introduce this activity with a statement such as:

> An empowerment-based relationship between a supervisor and worker shares much in common with a worker-family relationship. Here's an adaptation of the FDC Core Principles specifically for supervisors and leaders.

Read (or ask for volunteers to read) the *FDC Core Principles adapted for supervisors and leaders* slide (S4) and/or distribute the handout (H3).

> This is a walkabout activity similar to Stand by Your Quote from Chapter 1. The eleven principles are posted around the room. Walk around and read them again, selecting one that resonates with you the most. Discuss why this resonates with you and how you see this implemented at your organization with others who have selected the same principle.

Allow enough time for everyone to select a principle and have a small group discussion. Then, bring the group back together, still standing at their selected principles and ask them to share what was discussed for each one.

In closing, facilitate a brief discussion using this question:

> Many of the FDC Core Principles present an ideal or vision for what we'd like to have happen in our agency. What is one thing you could do to transform any one of these principles into a reality?

H3 The FDC Core Principles adapted for supervisors and leaders

1. All supervisors, staff members, and colleagues have strengths.

2. All supervisors and staff members need and deserve support in the work environment. The type and degree of support needed varies throughout the span of employment.

3. Most successful staff members are not dependent on long-term supervision. Neither are they independent in their functioning. They maintain healthy interdependence with their colleagues, supervisors, staff members and collaborators.

4. Diversity (race, ethnicity, gender, class, family form, religion, physical and mental ability, sexual orientation) is important and valuable in the workplace. Staff members need to develop competence in working effectively with people who may be different from themselves or who belong to groups that are not respected in our society.

5. The deficit model of supervision—in which staff members must show performance problems in order to receive supervision and in which the supervisor decides what is best for staff members—is counterproductive to helping them move toward healthy self-reliance.

6. Changing to a strengths-based model of supervision requires a new way of thinking about the supervisory relationship. Supervisors cannot make this shift without corresponding changes in how they work with their department heads or more senior administrators.

7. Staff members need a consistent approach in which all departments use a similar supervisory philosophy. Collaboration between departments is crucial to agency functioning. Staff members who feel disempowered within their departments collaborate less successfully than those who feel their strengths are valued.

8. Supervisors and staff members are equally important partners in the supervisory process, with each contributing important knowledge. Supervisors learn as much as staff members from the process.

9. Staff members must participate in setting their own goals and methods of achieving them. Supervisory roles include assisting staff members in setting reachable goals for their own self-reliance and performance, providing access to resources needed to reach those goals, and offering encouragement.

10. Supervision is provided for staff members to reach their goals, and is not, in itself, a measure of success. New methods of training and evaluating supervisors and staff members are needed to measure the outcomes and effectiveness of the supervisory relationship, not just the number of interactions.

11. For staff members to feel valued and committed, the supervisory system must shift from a "power over" to a "shared power" paradigm. Supervisors have power because they participate in the distribution of valued resources (status, promotion, recognition). Supervisors can use those resources to support staff members, rather than using them to exert power over workers.

1. All supervisors, staff members, and colleagues have strengths.

2. All supervisors and staff members need and deserve support in the work environment. The type and degree of support needed varies throughout the span of employment.

3. Most successful staff members are not dependent on long-term supervision. Neither are they independent in their functioning. They maintain healthy interdependence with their colleagues, supervisors, other staff members, and collaborators.

4. Diversity (race, ethnicity, gender, class, family form, religion, physical and mental ability, sexual orientation) is important and valuable in the workplace. Staff members need to develop competence in working effectively with people who may be different from themselves or who belong to groups that are not respected in our society.

5. The deficit model of supervision—in which staff members must show performance problems in order to receive supervision and in which the supervisor decides what is best for staff members—is counterproductive to helping them move toward healthy self-reliance.

6. Changing to a strengths-based model of supervision requires a new way of thinking about the supervisory relationship. Supervisors cannot make this shift without corresponding changes in how they work with their department heads and more senior administrators.

7. Staff members need a consistent approach in which all departments use a similar supervisory philosophy. Collaboration between departments is crucial to agency functioning. Staff members who feel disempowered collaborate less successfully than those who feel their strengths are valued.

8. Supervisors and staff members are equally important partners in the supervisory process, with each contributing important knowledge. Supervisors learn as much as staff members from the process.

9. Staff members must participate in setting their own goals and methods of achieving them. Supervisory roles include assisting staff members in setting reachable goals for their own self-reliance and performance, providing access to resources needed to reach those goals, and offering encouragement.

10. Supervision is provided for staff members to reach their goals, and is not, in itself, a measure of success. New methods of training and evaluating supervisors and staff members are needed to measure the outcomes and effectiveness of the supervisory relationship, not just the number of interactions.

11. For staff members to feel valued and committed, the supervisory system must shift from a "power over" to a "shared power" paradigm. Supervisors have power because they participate in the distribution of valued resources (status, promotion, recognition). Supervisors can use those resources to support staff members rather than using them to exert power over workers.

6. Models of effective supervision (30–45 min.)

Introduce this topic with a statement such as:

Chapter 2 describes the differences between two models of supervision, Transactional and Interactional and discusses the costs and benefits.

Review the *Transactional supervision* (S5), *Interactional supervision* (S6), and *What's the difference?* (S7) slides, covering the following points:

- Transactional supervision is more consistent with the "deficit" approach to family support; interactional supervision reflects principles of the empowerment-based approach.

- Transactional supervision assumes relationships are governed by "cause-effect" or reactive behaviors; interactional supervision recognizes that relationships are shaped by "reciprocal influences."

- Transactional supervision is based on the faulty assumption that supervisors must "fix" and provide incentives and pressures to change a worker's behavior. Interactional supervision is based on supervisors and workers working together to identify goals and solve problems.

On easel paper, write the heading "Interactional supervision" and make two columns labeled "Benefits" and "Costs." Do the same for "Transactional supervision," also making two columns labeled "benefits" and "costs." Have the group brainstorm ideas for each column. Ask if someone would like to share an example of a supervisory situation and how the situation might be handled using each approach.

Discuss the situation briefly, helping the group recognize the differences based on the example. Summarize the discussion emphasizing that the Interactional model of supervision aligns well with the family development approach.

Another model of supervision that aligns well with the family development approach is called Developmental supervision. In this model, a supervisor tailors the supervisory relationship using their assessment of the worker's need for direction, education, collaboration, or support.

Review the *Four approaches of Developmental supervision* slide (S8), covering the following points:

- Supervisors use the four approaches flexibly in working with a staff member or team. Note these are similar roles of a family development worker—not necessarily done in order or using all roles.

- The goal of supervision is to help workers develop their capacity for responsibility and interdependence.

- Level of supervision is based on helping a worker practice the skills needed for healthy self-reliance.

On easel paper, write the heading "Developmental supervision" and make two columns labeled "Benefits" and "Costs." Have the group brainstorm ideas for each column. Ask if someone would like to share an example of a supervisory situation that might be handled using Developmental supervision. Discuss the situation briefly, identifying the differences between the benefits and costs.

Continue with:

> **Reflective leadership focuses on learning to be present, to be aware and attentive to our experiences and interactions with people throughout the day. Reflective leadership is characterized by three important skills.**

Review the *Reflective leadership skills* slide (S9).

Summarize by saying that strategies to enhance Reflective leadership skills will be covered in Chapter 3, Leadership and Self-empowerment.

7.   Servant and Connective Leadership (30 min.)

Introduce this topic with a statement such as:

> Two other broad-based leadership approaches that align well with family development are servant leadership and connective leadership.

> Research to uncover the essential elements of effective leadership has increased dramatically. Advances in technology, the fluctuating economy, and the diverse composition of today's workforce have all affected the definition of what makes an effective leader. In the past, leadership was often defined simply as the opposite of followership. Here are some of the essentials of effective leadership today:

Review the *Characteristics of effective leadership* slide (S10).

> Servant leadership demonstrates the importance of recognizing individual strengths and how we integrate these attributes into what we do, and the overall impact. Let's look at the qualities of servant leadership as compared with the roles of a family development worker.

Review the *Qualities of servant leadership* slide (S11).

> Another broad-based style of leadership is called *connective* leadership. Here are the qualities of connective leaders compared with some of the Core Principles of family development.

Review the *Qualities of connective leaders* slide (S12).

> To explore the similarities and differences between servant-leaders and connective leaders in the day-to-day challenges of leadership, we're going to divide into two groups. One side of the room will have a discussion based on servant leadership; the other side on connective leadership. You are welcome to choose either group.

> Each group will have a sheet of easel paper to brainstorm ways each type of leadership style would demonstrate the qualities (essentials) of leadership we discussed earlier. I'll put the Qualities of effective leadership slide back up. Then, each group will generate a list of ways that a leader using that leadership approach would approach each task. For example, effective leaders need to be able to attract, inspire and retain workers in times of social, political and economic change. One group will generate a list of ways that a leader who uses servant leadership would accomplish that task. The other group will generate a list of ways a leader who uses connective leadership would accomplish that task. You'll have about 10 minutes to work on the list and you'll need to designate a spokesperson to share your ideas with the group when we reconvene.

Designate sides of the room for discussions on servant and connective leadership. Provide each group with easel paper and markers. If one group is larger than the other, ask the group to equalize the members so there is opportunity for all to share their ideas.

After 10 minutes, ask the group's spokesperson to share their ideas with the group. After both groups have presented, facilitate a brief discussion using the following question:

> **What similarities do you see in ways each leader might approach each task? What are some differences?**

Conclude the discussion with the idea that theories of supervision and leadership continue to evolve. Make a bridge to the next topic and activity by saying that most leaders have a personal leadership style and vision that influences their approach as well.

8.   What's your Leadership Style? (30–60 min.)

This section offers two different activities you can use with the group to help them reflect on their personal leadership style. You may choose to do one or both depending on available time.

One is Lipman-Blumen's "Description of Leadership Styles." Introduce this activity with a statement such as:

> If someone asked you to describe yourself as a leader, you'd probably start by listing some qualities of leadership you value or recount what others have told you about your leadership style.

The *Recognizing your leadership styles* worksheet (H4) is located on page 36 in the *Empowerment Skills for Leaders* handbook (or make copies and distribute). Ask the group to review the various leadership styles on page 35 and respond to the statements on the worksheet. Each style focuses on a leader's individual strengths. After allowing enough time to complete their responses, process the activity with discussion using these questions:

1. Did you find that you use similar leadership styles with most groups, or do you use a lot of different styles?

2. What are the advantages of using different leadership styles? What are the potential disadvantages?

Conclude the discussion by saying that leadership styles often change over time and can vary depending on the circumstances and/or the individuals they are supervising.

As an alternative or addition to the Lipman-Blumen activity, "The Leadership Compass" is an activity that not only helps leaders reflect on their own leadership style but helps them to appreciate those who have different styles and raises awareness of how to work more cooperatively with them.

Introduce the Leadership Compass activity with a statement such as:

> The Leadership Compass draws from a Native American–based practice called the Medicine Wheel or the Four-Fold Way. The four directions are described as warrior (north), healer (south), teacher (west) and visionary (east). There are other descriptors sometimes used for each direction that are more in line with human services such as action (north), empathy (south), analysis (west), and vision (east). All directions have profound strengths and potential weaknesses, and every person is seen as capable of growing in each direction.

> This activity can help us to:

- Deepen our appreciation of everyone's different work styles

- Understand the need for a variety of work styles

- Reflect on our own Individual work styles and opportunities for growth.

- Understand both positive and negative aspects of each style taken to excess.

- Learn the qualities we can develop to become better leaders and work effectively with others.

Distribute the *Leadership Compass Approaches to Work/Work Style* handouts (H5), and review or ask for volunteers to review the characteristics and potential weaknesses of each direction. Designate four areas of the room, one for each direction and ask leaders to move to the direction they feel best reflects their leadership style. Reinforce that it's unlikely anyone fits perfectly into only one, but for this activity, choose the one that fits the best.

After the groups have formed, ask them to discuss with each other why they selected that direction along with the plusses and minuses of those characteristics. After a few minutes, process the activity, giving each group an opportunity to share.

Conclude with discussion, using the following questions:

1. Why is it helpful to have team members with a variety of work styles?

2. How does having an awareness of your own leadership style help you to work more cooperatively with others?

H4 Worksheet: Recognizing your leadership styles

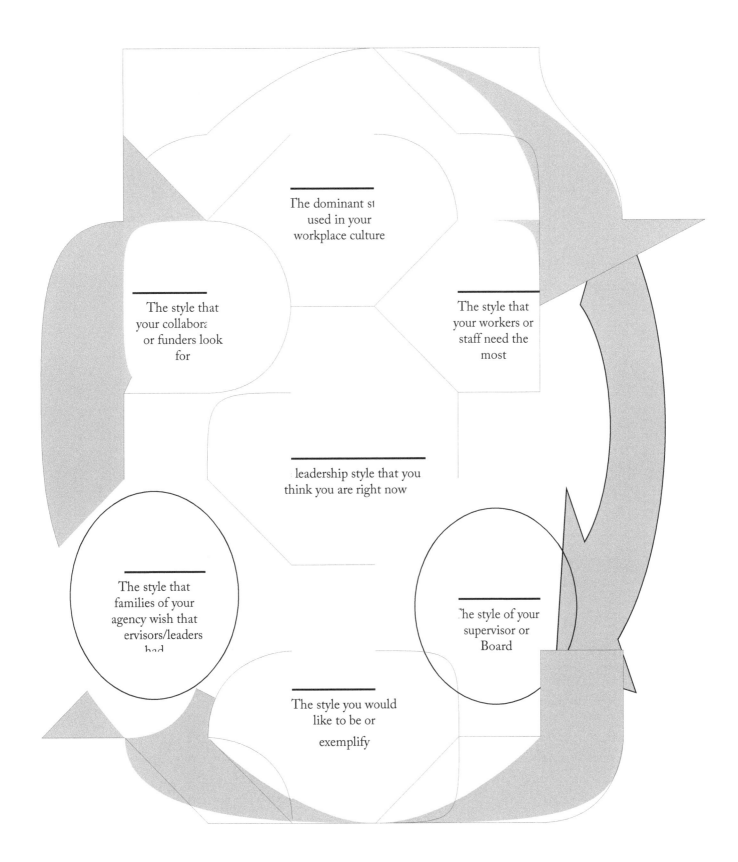

The dominant style used in your workplace culture

The style that your collaborators or funders look for

The style that your workers or staff need the most

leadership style that you think you are right now

The style that families of your agency wish that supervisors/leaders had

The style of your supervisor or Board

The style you would like to be or exemplify

NORTH
(Results)

Approaches to Work/ Work Style:
> - Assertive, active, decisive
> - Likes to determine course of events and be in control of professional relationship
> - Enjoys challenges presented by difficult situations and people
> - Thinks in terms of "bottom line"
> - Quick to act or decide; expresses urgency for others to take action
> - Perseveres, not stopped by hearing "No," probes and presses to get at hidden resistances
> - Likes variety, novelty, new projects
> - Comfortable being in front
> - Values action-oriented phrases, "Do it now!", "I'll do it", "What's the bottom line?"

Overuse: Style Taken to Excess:
> - Can easily overlook process and comprehensive strategic planning when driven by need to act and decide
> - Can get defensive, argue, try to "out expert" others
> - Can lose patience, pushes for decision before its time, avoids discussion
> - Can be autocratic, want things their way, has difficulty being a team member
> - Sees things in terms of black and white, not much tolerance for ambiguity
> - May go beyond limits, get impulsive, disregard practical issues
> - Not heedful of others' feelings, may be perceived as cold
> - Has trouble relinquishing control - find it hard to delegate, "If you want something done right, do it yourself!"

Best Ways to work with a North:
> - Present your case quickly, clearly, and with enthusiasm and confidence
> - Let them know they will be involved – their pay off and their role
> - Focus on the "challenge" of the task
> - Provide them with plenty of autonomy
> - Establish timelines and stick with them
> - Give them positive, public recognition
> - Use them to complete tasks that require motivation, persuasion, and initiative

Leadership Compass – Appreciating Diverse Work styles
Resources taken from the Bonner Foundation
Adapted by RDH, 10/14/06, from:
http://nationalserviceresources.org/filemanager/download/06_MultiState_Conf/14LeadershipCompass-Participantshandout.doc

4

SOUTH
(Relationships)

Approaches to Work/ Work Style:
> ➤ Understands how people need to receive information in order to act on it
> ➤ Integrates others input in determining direction of what's happening
> ➤ Value-driven regarding aspects of professional life
> ➤ Uses professional relationships to accomplish tasks, interaction is a primary way of getting things done
> ➤ Supportive to colleagues and peers
> ➤ Willingness to trust others' statements at face value
> ➤ Feeling-based, trusts own emotions and intuition, intuition regarded as "truth"
> ➤ Receptive to other's ideas, builds on ideas, team player, noncompetitive
> ➤ Able to focus on the present
> ➤ Values words like "right" and "fair"

Overuse: Style Taken to Excess:
> ➤ Can lose focus on goals when believes relationships or people's needs are being compromised
> ➤ Has trouble saying "No" to requests
> ➤ Internalizes difficulty and assumes blame
> ➤ Prone to disappointment when relationship is seen as secondary to task
> ➤ Difficulty confronting or handling anger (own or others'); may be manipulated by emotions
> ➤ Can over-compromise in order to avoid conflict
> ➤ Immersed in the present or now; loses track of time; may not take action or see long-range view
> ➤ Can become too focused on the process, at the expense of accomplishing goals

Best Ways to Work with a South:
> ➤ Remember process, attention to what is happening with the relationship between you
> ➤ Justify your decisions around values and ethics
> ➤ Appeal your relationship with this person and his or her other relationships
> ➤ Listen hard and allow the expression of feelings and intuition in logical arguments
> ➤ Be aware that this person may have a hard time saying "NO" and may be easily steamrolled
> ➤ Provide plenty of positive reassurance and likeability
> ➤ Let the person know you like them and appreciate them

Leadership Compass – Appreciating Diverse Work styles
Resources taken from the Bonner Foundation
Adapted by RDH, 10/14/06, from:
http://nationalserviceresources.org/filemanager/download/06_MultiState_Conf/14LeadershipCompass-Participantshandout.doc

EAST
(Vision)

Approaches to Work/ Work Style:
> ➢ Visionary who sees the big picture
> ➢ Generative and creative thinker, able to think outside the box
> ➢ Very idea-oriented; focuses on future thought
> ➢ Makes decisions by standing in the future (insight/imagination)
> ➢ Insight into mission and purpose
> ➢ Looks for overarching themes, ideas
> ➢ Adept at and enjoys problem solving
> ➢ Likes to experiment, explore
> ➢ Appreciates a lot of information
> ➢ Values words like "option," "possibility," "imagine"

Overuse: Style Taken to Excess:
> ➢ Can put too much emphasis on vision at the expense of action or details
> ➢ Can lose focus on tasks
> ➢ Poor follow through on projects, can develop a reputation for lack of dependability and attention to detail
> ➢ Not time-bound, may lose track of time
> ➢ Tends to be highly enthusiastic early on, then burn out over the long haul
> ➢ May lose interest in projects that do not have a comprehensive vision
> ➢ May find self frustrated and overwhelmed when outcomes are not in ling with vision

Best ways to work with an East:
> ➢ Show appreciation and enthusiasm for ideas
> ➢ Listen and be patient during idea generation
> ➢ Avoid criticizing or judging ideas
> ➢ Allow and support divergent thinking
> ➢ Provide a variety of tasks
> ➢ Provide help and supervision to support detail and project follow through

Leadership Compass – Appreciating Diverse Work styles
Resources taken from the Bonner Foundation
Adapted by RDH, 10/14/06, from:
http://nationalserviceresources.org/filemanager/download/06_MultiState_Conf/I4LeadershipCompass-Participantshandout.doc

WEST
(Process)

Approaches to Work/ Work Style:
> ➢ Understands what information is needed to assist in decision making
> ➢ Seen as practical, dependable and thorough in task situations
> ➢ Provides planning and resources, is helpful to others in these ways and comes through for the team
> ➢ Moves carefully and follows procedures and guidelines
> ➢ Uses data analysis and logic to make decisions
> ➢ Weighs all sides of an issue, balanced
> ➢ Introspective, self-analytical, critical thinker
> ➢ Skilled at finding fatal flaws in an idea or project
> ➢ Maximizes existing resources - gets the most out of what has been done in the past
> ➢ Values word like "objective" "analysis"

Overuse: Style Taken to Excess:
> ➢ Can be bogged down by information, doing analysis at the expense of moving forward
> ➢ Can become stubborn and entrenched in position
> ➢ Can be indecisive, collect unnecessary data, mired in details, "analysis paralysis"
> ➢ May appear cold, withdrawn, with respect to others' working styles
> ➢ Tendency toward remaining on the sidelines, watchfulness, observation
> ➢ Can become distanced
> ➢ May be seen as insensitive to others' emotions or resistant to change

Best Ways to Work with a West:
> ➢ Allow plenty of time for decision-making
> ➢ Provide data-objective facts and figures that a West can trust
> ➢ Don't be put off by critical "NO" statements
> ➢ Minimize the expression of emotion and use logic when possible
> ➢ Appeal to tradition, a sense of history, and correct procedures.

9.   Recognizing the natural assets of your staff members and organization (40 min.)

Activity: What's going right?

Introduce this activity with a statement such as:

> An important element of using a family development approach is the capacity to see the reality of a situation while looking deeply at your organization's strengths even when things aren't going so well. This is a quote from a leader who participated in an FDC Leadership focus group. This quote reflects the challenge of focusing on strengths even during times of crisis in your agency:

Read the *"What's going right?" focus group quote* slide (S13) (or ask a volunteer to read):

> A leader at an FDC Leadership focus group said:

> "You have the sense of the (strengths-based) philosophy and then it's so easy to fall off the wagon, to not incorporate it on a daily basis. As a supervisor, often a staff member is talking to you about a crisis situation, and you come at it in your crisis mode. It's hard to stop and regroup and remember to ask that one question: 'What is going right?'"

Ask participants to work in pairs and share examples of "what's going right" in their organizations right now. Allow enough time for discussion and reconvene the group asking for volunteers to share some of their examples.

Follow with a brief discussion using these questions:

---

1. Why is focusing on "What's going right" a good place to start in making the paradigm shift from "power over" to "shared power?"

2. In what ways can supervisors and leaders regroup and refocus on strengths during a crisis?

Activity: Helping staff members build on their strengths (20 min.)

In advance, write one of the following worker's characteristics on a separate sheet of easel paper. Then post the sheets around the room. If the group is small or time is short, post fewer sheets.

1. Is new and unfamiliar with the organization

2. Has been there a long time and "seen it all"

3. Is very private about their life

4. Shares too much about their life

5. Is always willing to try new things

6. Has physical challenges or limited mobility

7. Resists doing things differently

8. Always comes through when you need them

9. Has chronic health challenges

10. Needs a lot of emotional support

11. Has future career goals in another field

12. Does just enough to get by

13. Is very productive, but frequently needs time off from work

14. Has a "strong" personality

15. Appears to let others "walk all over them"

16. Has a lot of knowledge through formal education

17. Has a lot of knowledge through personal experience

Introduce this activity by reviewing the *Recognizing the natural assets of employees* slide (S14), and with the following statement:

> **One of the most important skills you'll need as a leader is the ability to help staff members identify and build on their strengths. Let's review the following list of characteristics of staff members found in a typical organization:**

Distribute and read (or ask for volunteers to read) the *Helping staff members build on their strengths* worksheet (H6). Continue with:

> **Each of the characteristics we just reviewed is written on individual sheets around the room. Please take a pen or pencil with you and stand at one of the sheets.**

If the class has more than 15 participants, you can have two people stand and move together. Then continue:

> This is a quick-paced activity to generate ideas about strengths that come to mind about staff members. When I say "Go," you'll have about 10 seconds to think of and write a strength that goes with that characteristic on the sheet. Then, I'll say, "Switch" and you'll move to the next sheet on your right and have 10 seconds to think of and write a strength at that station. I'll say "Switch" about every 10 seconds, and you'll keep moving until you've written a strength for each characteristic. You can read the other strengths that are written, however, think of a new strength or different focus if you can. Are there any questions?

After you confirm that everyone is ready, say "Go." Then every 10 seconds or so, say "Switch." Keep the pace lively but accommodate the need for more time if necessary. After you see that participants have visited all the stations, go around asking them to read the sheet where they are standing.

The worksheet listing the characteristics we just discussed can help you reflect on your own staff members and the strengths they bring to the workplace.

Conclude the activity with a brief discussion using the following questions:

1. Based on your experience doing this activity, can you share a new idea or insight about a strength in a staff member you may know?

2. This activity highlights how staff members' strengths often complement each other. How could this knowledge be helpful for you and your organization?

H6 Worksheet: Helping staff members build on their strengths

Think of a strength of a staff member who....

1. Is new and unfamiliar with the organization _____

2. Has been there a long time and "seen it all" _____

3. Is very private about their life _____

4. Shares too much about their life _____

5. Is always willing to try new things _____

6. Has physical challenges or limited mobility _____

7. Resists doing things differently _____

8. Always comes through when you need them _____

9. Has chronic health challenges _____

10. Needs a lot of emotional support _____

11. Has future career goals in another field _____

12. Does just enough to get by _____

13. Is very productive, but frequently needs time off from work _____

14. Has a "strong" personality _____

15. Appears to let others "walk all over them" _____

16. Has a lot of knowledge through formal education _____

17. Has a lot of knowledge through personal experience _____

10. Aligning your leadership vision with the mission of the organization (30 min.)

Introduce this topic with a statement such as:

> A mission statement sends an important message to the community about the services and support your agency provides, and the outcomes it seeks to achieve. Aligning your leadership vision with the mission of the organization helps translate that message into a plan of action. Picture a ladder that leans against a wall for someone to climb. Your leadership vision is the first step of the ladder that aligns with the mission of the organization at the highest rung. Your leadership vision starts with beliefs, thoughts, and actions that are set into motion to achieve objectives, goals, and outcomes. Let's look at a graphic of how the process might occur.

Review the *Aligning your vision with the mission of the organization* slide (S15).

Distribute copies of the *Aligning your vision with the mission of the organization* worksheet (H7). Ask participants to write or paraphrase their agency's mission in the top of the sheet. Then, either individually or working with a partner from their organization, starting with the bottom rung, ask them to develop the continuum of statements on the worksheet that proceed from their vision and end with the agency's mission.

After 10 minutes, ask the group to reconvene and invite sharing if the group is comfortable doing so. Then, facilitate a brief discussion using these questions:

1. What type of things can get in the way of aligning your leadership vision with the mission of your agency?

2. What can a leader do when the organization's message to families or employees (an attitude, belief, or value expressed in policies or practice) appears to conflict with the mission of the organization?

H7 Worksheet: Aligning your vision with the mission of the organization

Write the actual or a paraphrased mission statement of your organization. Then complete the steps from 1 to 6 to align your leadership vision by writing your response in each rung of the ladder.

Mission of your organization: _____

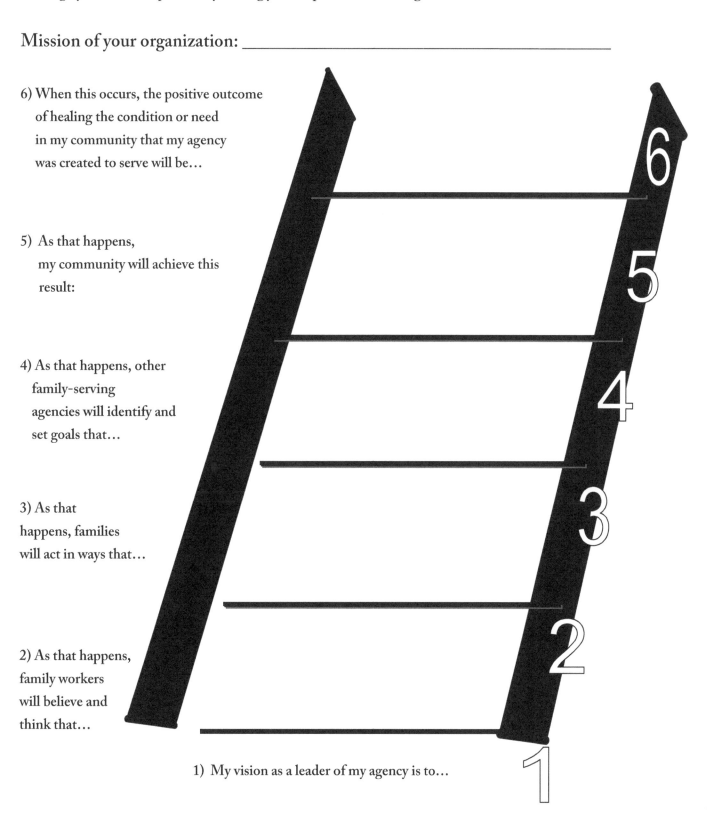

6) When this occurs, the positive outcome of healing the condition or need in my community that my agency was created to serve will be…

5) As that happens, my community will achieve this result:

4) As that happens, other family-serving agencies will identify and set goals that…

3) As that happens, families will act in ways that…

2) As that happens, family workers will believe and think that…

1) My vision as a leader of my agency is to…

11. The Workplace Empowerment Plan (60 min.)

In advance of this activity, make copies of the *Workplace Empowerment Plan role play* sheet (H8) to have sufficient parts for each group.

Introduce this activity with a statement such as:

> The Workplace Empowerment Plan is an adaptation of the Family Development Plan currently used by workers in family-serving agencies across the country. The purpose of the workplace empowerment plan is to help supervisors, leaders, and staff members identify a goal for greater empowerment in the workplace and work collaboratively to achieve that goal together. Here are some short-term goals that leaders and staff members might work on together:

Review (or ask volunteers to read) the *Short-term goals for workplace empowerment* handout (H9).

> Here is a sample of the Workplace Empowerment Plan Form that is also found in Chapter 2 of the Empowerment Skills for Leaders Handbook.

Distribute and review the *Workplace Empowerment Plan* handout (H10).

> In this activity, you'll practice developing a Workplace Empowerment Plan in a group of five people. I'll give each person in the group a slip of paper that describes the role you'll play. Each group will have a piece of easel paper to develop their plan based on the example.
>
> The group needs to select a member to record the information and designate a spokesperson to present the plan to the entire group. You'll have about 20 minutes to work on the plan; it's OK if you don't finish. Are there any questions?

Help arrange the class into groups with five members. Pass out one role-play slip to each person. Give each group easel paper and marker. Circulate around the room during the activity to answer questions and provide encouragement. After about 20 minutes, invite each group's spokesperson to present the group's work.

Facilitate a brief discussion using these questions:

1. How does this process compare with a traditional approach in which a leader or group of supervisors develop a plan to achieve a goal?

2. What might you need to do to use this goal-setting process in your workplace?

H8 Workplace Empowerment Plan role play

You are an employee who is new to the agency and feels overwhelmed with the amount of work to do each week. You want to ask for regularly scheduled meetings with your supervisor and other co-workers to learn how they manage their time and duties.

You are a worker who has been with the agency for ten years. You are skeptical that a Workplace Empowerment Plan is just another management technique the organization will start, but not follow through on. You are open to whatever goal the group decides on but want the plan to reflect that both leaders and staff have shared responsibility for the goal.

You are the supervisor of a family program. You would like the group to develop the goal of using a team-oriented approach to serve families and achieve the outcomes of your program. You are willing to defer your idea to a later date if the group has a more pressing goal to address.

You are the director of a large department. You are there to support the group in developing a doable plan. You want to help staff members to feel that their work is valued by the agency. Based on budget review, you are willing to allocate the necessary time and resources needed to achieve the goal they set.

You are a worker who has recently transferred to this program from another department. The department you previously worked in used an innovative approach in supporting families—two family workers worked together with a pre-set number of families. You'd like the group to consider this idea and schedule a meeting with your former colleagues to learn more about their duties and outcomes.

H9 Short-term goals for workplace empowerment

1. Recognize and appreciate each staff member's talents and abilities.

2. Help staff members put new skills to use.

3. Provide orientation and training to enhance job performance.

4. Provide the resources needed to do a job well (e.g. time, equipment,

5. supplies, information).

6. Set manageable timeframes for getting work done.

7. Support and help workers in prioritizing tasks.

8. Help with reprioritizing tasks to accomplish time-sensitive work.

9. Give regular feedback and encouragement to staff members.

10. Offer support and help when unanticipated problems occur.

11. Solicit input and feedback from staff members.

12. Offer praise and acknowledgement when goals are achieved.

13. Provide a balance of challenge and routine in job tasks.

14. Build a sense of community within the organization.

15. Recognize ways that individuals and teams make important contributions.

16. Develop methods through which teams can offer support to one another.

17. Develop new working relationships with other teams or departments.

Additional goals

18. _____

19. _____

20. _____

21. _____

22. _____

23. _____

24. _____

25. _____

26. _____

H10 Workplace Empowerment Plan for _____

(agency or program name)

Today's date: _____

Supervisor and Staff Members involved in this workplace empowerment process:

_____

_____

Short-term goal:

_____

Steps leading to this goal:

Steps the supervisor will take and when:

_____

_____

_____

Steps workers and staff members will take and when:

_____

_____

_____

Natural assets and strengths (staff members, supervisor, co-workers, and others in the organization):

_____

_____

_____

Concerns (staff members, supervisor, co-workers, and others in the organization):

_____

_____

_____

Services and resources available: (including names, addresses, phone numbers, etc.)

_____

_____

_____

Date, time, and location to review progress:

_____

Names of people who will attend progress meeting:

_____

_____

12. Assessing the level of empowerment in your workplace (30 min.)

Introduce this topic with a statement such as:

> The term "empowerment" has a specific meaning and context in family development. Here is how empowerment is defined in the family development model.

Read (or ask for a volunteer to read) the *Definition of empowerment in family development* slide (S16).

> Empowerment is an experience that comes from within. Workers can't "empower" families, and in turn, supervisors and leaders can't empower staff members. What you can do as a supervisor and leader is to develop mutually respectful relationships with staff members and collaborate with them on achieving goals of healthy self-reliance in the workplace.
>
> Sometimes there are circumstances outside your control that interfere with developing mutually respectful relationships and collaborating on empowerment-based goals. For example, a family worker can feel torn between their belief in empowering families and the need to enforce organizational policies or regulations that may result in denial or withdrawal of a family's services. Experiencing this conflict between two competing belief or value systems is called "dissonance." Here are some of the ways people try to reconcile this dissonance.

Review the *Conflict between competing beliefs* (S17) and *Ways workers try to reconcile a conflict between competing beliefs* (S18) slides.

> Here are two situations where a conflict could arise between an organization's policies and practices and a worker's belief or value system.

Read (or ask for a volunteer to read) the first example on the *Situations to assess the level of empowerment in your workplace* worksheet (H11).

> Referring to the first case situation, help the group generate a list of the potential organizational policies or practices, beliefs and values a worker might have about the situation, and how a supervisor or leader could help.
>
> Explain that there may be no right or wrong answers, but that understanding the potential for a conflict between competing values and belief systems can be helpful in assessing the level of empowerment in their workplace.

Ask group members to choose a partner and ask them to discuss the second situation for about 10 minutes and respond to the same three areas (organizational policies and practices, worker's beliefs and values, how a supervisor or leader can help).

After about 10 minutes, ask the group to reconvene. Facilitate a brief discussion using these questions:

---

1. Why is it important for supervisors and leaders to understand the concept of dissonance and how it affects staff members in their organization?

2. How could you assess the level of empowerment in your workplace?

H11 Worksheet: Situations to assess the level of empowerment in your workplace

	Organizational policy or practice	Worker's belief or value	How a supervisor or leader can help
Situation 1: A family is denied program services because their income just exceeds eligibility requirements.			
Situation 2: A worker must end a relationship with a family because achieving the family's goal makes them no longer eligible for the agency's services.			

13.   Building your agency's capacity for transformation (20 min.)

Introduce this topic with a statement such as:

> Over time, all organizations experience transitions; while some of them may be predictable and welcome, others can be sudden or unexpected, and put an agency into crisis. Chapter 2 presents three types of change in organizations.

Review the *Three types of change in organizations* slide (S19).

Facilitate a discussion using these questions:

---

1.   How does each type of change affect the relationship between a supervisor and employee?

2.   If your agency decided to create a new organizational culture using family development principles and practices, what would need to happen? Write these ideas on easel paper.

Read (or ask for volunteers to read) the *Guidelines for building your agency's capacity for transformation* slide (S20).

Continue the discussion with the idea that transformational change can extend to other major organizational changes such as reorganization, merger, or acquisition. Ask group members if anyone has ever experienced transformational change in an organization, and if they would like to share a reflection on the experience. Thank those who volunteer to share.

Facilitate the discussion in a way that helps participants recognize that transformational change in organizations requires two components not typically found in developmental and transitional change: preparation and reflection. Try to help the group understand these differences without presenting the ideas yourself, but rather by helping them come to understand these differences through discussion of their experiences.

14.   "Talking the talk" and "walking the walk" (30 min.)

Introduce this activity with a statement such as:

> In FDC training, workers learn that to "talk the talk" and "walk the walk" means to become actively involved in helping their organizations apply the philosophy and practices of family development. In a family development workplace, everyone benefits from shared knowledge and expertise.

> To "talk the talk" and "walk the walk" as a leader, you need to continuously assess and reassess opportunities and challenges. Using principles of empowerment-based assessment, you won't need to continually rationalize or re-strategize every decision. When you make decisions based on ongoing assessment that focuses on families' and staff members' strengths, you are using empowerment-based assessment. Here are FDC's six basic principles of empowerment-based assessment.

Review the *Principles of empowerment-based assessment* slide (S21).

> Agency forms and procedures can work against the family development process if they reflect a deficit-oriented rather than an empowerment approach. Some forms and procedures may be outdated, but still in use because they haven't been reviewed since the agency adopted principles of family development.

> In this activity, we'll divide into groups of three. As a group, you'll develop a hypothetical intake form, incorporating the principles of empowerment-based assessment. Each group will write their ideas on easel paper and designate a spokesperson to share with the entire group. You'll have about 10 minutes to work on this.

After about 10 minutes, ask the group to reconvene inviting each group's spokesperson to present their ideas.

Thank each group for their ideas and review the *Guidelines for developing empowerment-based assessment tools* slide (S22). Facilitate a brief discussion using this question:

> **How do families benefit when an agency uses empowerment-based assessment?**

Conclude discussion with the idea that adopting more family-focused and outcomes-based program assessment tools requires that supervisors and leaders work collaboratively with funders to come up with innovative ways to develop and revise reporting forms. Encourage them *not* to think of "family-focused" and "outcomes-based" as opposites, but rather as essential and integral components of the process of demonstrating a program's impact on families and the community.

15.   Planning Independent Learning Projects (30 min.)

Invite participants to spend a few minutes thinking about an Independent Learning Project that will demonstrate what they have learned in this chapter.

Ask them to find a partner with whom they will alternate the role of peer advisor and advisee. Ask them to get together, each discussing their plans. Then, ask them to write their plan on the form. Encourage them to support each other in setting a manageable plan and time frame to complete their projects.

16.   Quick Feedback form (10 min.)

Thank people for their time and participation in coming to the session. In advance, make enough copies of the feedback form. Remind them that the feedback is extremely important and that you'll summarize the overall comments at the next session.

Empowerment Skills for Leaders

Chapter 2: Transforming your Workplace through Empowerment-Based Leadership

Quick Feedback Form

When during the session did you feel most engaged?

When during the session did you feel least engaged?

What would make your experience in this course better?

Thanks for your feedback!

Chapter 2 PowerPoint slides

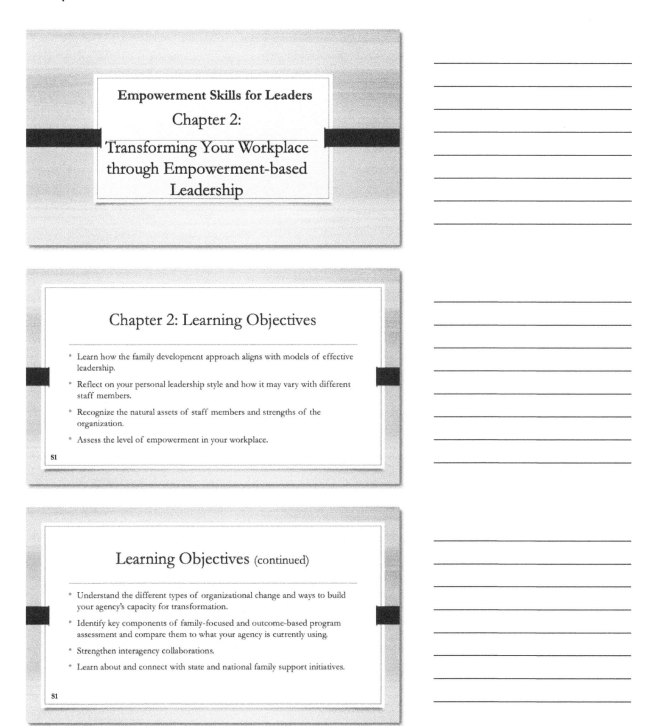

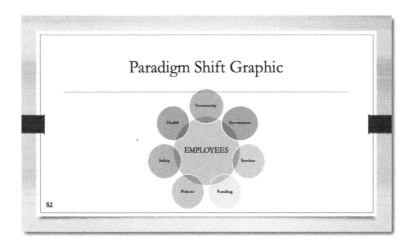

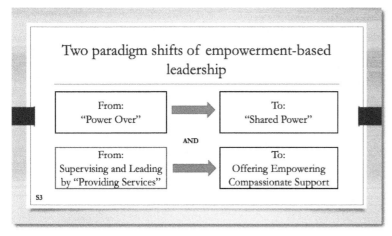

FDC Core Principles adapted for supervisors and leaders

1. All supervisors, staff members and colleagues have strengths.

2. All supervisors and staff members need and deserve support in the work environment. The type and degree of support needed varies throughout the span of employment.

3. Most successful staff members are not dependent on everyday supervision, neither are they independent in their functioning. They maintain healthy interdependence with their colleagues, supervisors and collaborators.

S4

FDC Core Principles (continued)

4. Diversity (race, ethnicity, gender, class, family form, religion, physical and mental ability, sexual orientation) is important and valuable in the workplace. Supervisors need to develop competence in working effectively with staff who may be different from themselves, or who belong to groups not respected in society.

5. The deficit model of supervision, in which staff members must show performance problems to receive supervision, and in which the supervisor decides what's best for staff members is counterproductive to helping them move toward healthy self-reliance.

6. Changing to a strength-based model of supervision requires a new way of thinking about the supervisory relationship. Supervisors cannot make this shift without corresponding changes in how they work with their department heads or more senior administrators.

S4

FDC Core Principles (continued)

7. Staff members need a consistent approach in which all departments use a similar supervisory philosophy. Collaboration between departments is crucial to agency functioning, and staff that feel disempowered collaborate less successfully than those whose strengths are valued.

8. Supervisors and staff members are equally important partners in the supervision process, with each contributing important knowledge. Supervisors learn as much as staff members from the process.

9. Staff members must participate in setting their own goals and methods of achieving them. Supervisory roles include assisting staff members in setting reachable goals for their performance and self-reliance, providing access to resources needed to reach their goals, and offering encouragement.

S4

FDC Core Principles (continued)

10. Supervision is provided for staff members to reach their goals and is not in itself a measure of success. New methods of training and evaluating supervisors and staff members are needed that measure outcomes and effectiveness of the supervisory partnership, not just the number of contacts.

11. For staff members to feel valued and committed, the supervisory system must shift from a "power over" to a "shared power" paradigm. Supervisors have power because they participate in the distribution of valued resources (status, promotion, recognition). They can then use those resources to support staff members, rather than exert power over them.

S4

Transactional supervision aligns with the "deficit" model of support

- Supervisors know what is best for employees ("power over").

- Unless closely monitored, employees will not be productive and will become lazy and dishonest.

- Employees will follow up on whatever is recommended.

S5

Interactional supervision aligns with the "empowerment" model of support

- Employees are most successful in accomplishing plans they create in consultation with their supervisor (shared power), not plans their supervisors make for them (power over).

- Supervisors see their role as assisting employees in recognizing their strengths and challenges.

- Supervisors support employees in accomplishing mutually agreed-upon goals.

S6

What's the Difference?

Transactional supervision assumes relationships are governed by "cause-effect" or reactive behaviors. *Interactional* supervision contends that relationships are shaped by "reciprocal influences".

Transactional supervision is based on the faulty assumption that supervisors must "fix" and provide incentives and pressures to change an employee's behavior. *Interactional* supervision is based on supervisors and employees working together to identify goals and solve problems.

Transactional and Interactional models of supervision were developed by Lawrence Shulman

S7

Four Approaches of Developmental Supervision

* Providing an appropriate level of direction for a worker to develop healthy autonomy
* Providing necessary information needed for a worker to act with responsibility
* Providing clarification, encouragement and guidance based on the assumption that a worker knows best what changes need to be made.
* Assisting workers with assessment and planning in a way that supports the worker individually, and at the organizational level.

S8   The Developmental model of supervision was developed by Carl Glickman, Stephen Gordon & Jovita Ross-Gordon

Reflective leadership skills

Self-awareness- knowing your own unique gifts and talents, along with your biases and limitations.

Careful observation- listening and figuring out the meaning behind what you see and hear.

Flexible responses- knowing the personal styles of employees, how they work best and what motivates them.

S9

Characteristics of effective leaders

* Ability to attract, inspire, and retain employees in times of social, political, and economic change.
* Capacity to collaboratively design and implement programs that meet community needs.
* Consistent ability to build the organization's cultural competence and cultural humility, teamwork, creativity, and meaningful collaborations.
* Able to nurture, support, collaborate, solve problems, make decisions and share power.
* Others?

S10

Qualities of a Servant Leader

* Aspires to lead by serving others
* Motivated by concern for the physical, emotional and spiritual well-being of others
* Builds relationships based on commitment and empathy
* Other characteristics include listening, awareness, persuasion, conceptualization, foresight, and building community

S11   The term "Servant Leader" was originally created by Robert Greenleaf

Qualities of a Connective Leader

* Builds cohesive relationships with others based on seeking out mutual problems and goals.
* Reaches out to former opponents to help implement grander visions in the community.
* Sees diversity as a valuable and necessary component of opportunity.
* Shares power as the way to empower others.
* Authenticity- "walking the walk" and accountability-transparency.

S12   The term and qualities of "connective leadership" were developed by Jean Lipman-Blumen

What's going right?

A leader at an FDC leadership focus group said:

"you have the sense of the (strengths-based) philosophy and then it's so easy to fall off the wagon, to not incorporate it on a daily basis. As a supervisor, often a staff member is talking to you about a crisis situation, and you come at it in your crisis mode. It's hard to stop, regroup and remember to ask that one question:"

What is going right?

S13

Recognizing the natural assets of your employees

One of the most important skills you'll need as a leader is the ability to help employees identify and build on their strengths.

Let's look at a list of employee characteristics found in a typical organization.

S14

Aligning your Leadership Vision with the Mission of the Organization

A mission statement sends an important message to the community about the services and support your organization provides, and the outcomes it seeks to achieve.

Your leadership vision is the first rung on the "ladder".

S15

Definition of "empowerment" in family development

Empowerment is a dynamic process through which leaders and staff members in organizations work with each other (and other organizations) to achieve goals that support family development in their communities.

Empowerment also means helping communities, states and the nation create the conditions through which families can reach their own goals, which may include changing human service systems.

S16

Conflict between "competing beliefs"

Dissonance is a state of mind that occurs when a person feels a conflict between two competing belief or value systems.

We use the term "competing beliefs" to describe an organization disconnected from its mission. For example, a supervisor may feel torn between providing empowerment-based support to a staff member and enforcing organizational policies or government regulations that don't align with those beliefs.

S17

Ways employees try to reconcile a conflict between competing beliefs

1) Shifting to the belief that empowerment-based support should be provided only under circumstances they feel are worthy.

2) Performing work duties with a "by the book" attitude and feeling stressed about having to act in a way that conflicts with their values.

3) Becoming trapped in "submission and aggression loop" relationships.

4) A combination of any or all the above. These conflicting feelings can have an impact on you, your co-workers and their own families.

S18

Three types of change in organizations

Developmental Change develops the skills and competencies of staff members so they can perform their jobs more effectively.

Impact: Increased productivity and more consistent achievement of outcomes.

Transitional Change combines efforts across the organization and effects multiple levels of operation and administration.

Impact: Less effective and outdated modes of operation are replaced with new and improved techniques.

S19

Three types of change in organizations (continued)

Transformational Change is broad-based change that alters the culture and practices of an organization that affect employees, customers, competitors and sometimes even the larger culture.

Impact: An ongoing process that delves beneath the surface of normal organizational practices and requires attentiveness to the impact of change itself on the organization.

There may be strong reactions, reservations and even resistance from some employees.

S19

Guidelines for building your organization's capacity for transformation

* Prepare your organization for transformational change in ways that help all employees appreciate and support one another.

* Offer opportunities for employees to reflect on the process of transformational change.

* Provide opportunities for employees to share their ideas and feelings about what's working well and what isn't.

S20

Principles of empowerment-based assessment "talking the talk" and "walking the walk"

1. Assessment is an ongoing process.
2. Focus on individual's strengths, current situation and future goals.
3. Effective assessment is person-driven.
4. Assessment *with* staff members is much more effective than assessment *for* them.
5. Collect only the information you need.
6. Assessment must be respectful and culturally appropriate.

S21

Guidelines for developing empowerment-based assessment/evaluation tools

- Empowerment-based assessment is process oriented- Based on the recognition that goals, needs and resources will change over time.

- Empowerment-based assessment is flexible- Conventional, standardized assessments typically emphasize broad-based outcomes and goals with little or no acknowledgement of multiple secondary goals achieved in the process.

- Empowerment-based assessment focuses on strengths- While it is important to accurately address performance issues, ongoing assessment should also provide space for the employee to indicate strengths and mutually defined goals.

S22

CHAPTER 3
LEADERSHIP AND SELF-EMPOWERMENT

Teaching materials

- LCD projector/smart board/power points
- Index cards
- Easel, easel paper, and markers
- Masking or cellophane tape
- Handouts and worksheets
- Melodic bell or chime (for reconvening the group)
- Supplemental resources (optional)
- Refreshments (optional)

	Activities	Approximate Duration (minutes)	Slides	Handouts/Materials
1	*Agenda and Ch. 2 Feedback Summary*	5		
2	*Ch. 3 Learning Objectives*	10	S1 Learning objectives for Ch. 3	
3	*Some of the toughest things about being a leader*	15		H1 "Some of the toughest things about being a leader" survey
4	*Recognizing your strengths as a supervisor and leader*	30		
5	*Clarifying a personal vision for your work*	30		H2 Worksheet: Clarifying your personal vision for work
6	*Shifting your focus from "doing" to "being"*	30		
7	*Mindful leadership*	30–45	S2 What is mindfulness? S3 Benefits of mindful leadership S4 Practical strategies for mindful leadership	
8	*Mindfulness exercises*	30–45		
9	*Removing distractions*	30		H3 Worksheet: Removing distractions
10	*Feeling good about the work you do*	30	S5 Feeling good about the work you do	
11	*Family Circles Assessment Adapted for Leaders*	30		H4 Family Circles Assessment Adapted for Leaders H5 Family Circles Adapted for Leaders Guide
12	*Balancing work and personal life*	30	S6 Ways to balance work and personal life	H6 Worksheet: Balancing your work and personal life
13	*Creating your own stress and wellness program*	30	S7 Effects of chronic stress on health and well-being S8 A potter's view of stress S9 Components of a personal stress reduction and wellness program	H7 Personal stress reduction and wellness calendar
14	*Planning an Independent Learning Project and the Leadership Empowerment Plan*	30		Leadership Empowerment Plan

Activities	Approximate Duration (minutes)	Slides	Handouts/Materials
16 *Quick Feedback Form*	10		Quick Feedback Form

Supplemental Resources

There are resources at the end of each chapter in the *Empowerment Skills for Leaders* Handbook. A suggestion would be to select one of the articles listed (or another of your choice) that you feel is relevant and of interest to the group and distribute copies for them to read (or refer them to a link online) before the next class session. At the beginning of the next class session, facilitate a brief discussion about the article and how it reinforces the concepts covered in the chapter.

Links to additional resources are on the FDC website, www.familydevelopmentcredential.org, under Instructor Resources.

Videos

Kabat Zinn, Jon. "Life is right now." https://www.youtube.com/watch?v=EU7vKitN4Ro.

"Let's Talk About Mindfulness: An Interview with Ellen Langer." https://www.youtube.com/watch?v=erUyCnm-9uY.

"Meet Richard Davidson." https://www.youtube.com/watch?v=hyJQ-UdUnkU.

"The Fish Philosophy—At the Pike Place Fish Market." Fishmongers identify four simple practices that help anyone bring new energy and commitment to their work. https://www.charthouselearning.com/.

UMass Center for Mindfulness. This website features a CBS 60 minutes segment featuring journalist Anderson Cooper's journey to mindfulness and the follow-up neuroscientific analysis conducted by Dr. Judson Brewer at the Center for Mindfulness. https://www.umassmed.edu/cfm/.

Podcasts

"Mindfulness: Finding Peace in a Frantic World." Free meditations. https://www.franticworld.com/.

University of California-Los Angeles (UCLA) Mindfulness Awareness Research Center. https://marc.ucla.edu/body.cfm?id=22.

Websites

Wellness and Stress Management Handouts:
https://www.umassmed.edu/psychiatry/wellness/stresshandouts.aspx
https://www.psychologytoday.com/us/basics/mindfulness
https://mindful.org/

Activities

1.   Agenda and Chapter 2 feedback summary (5 min.)

Welcome everyone back. Provide a short feedback summary from the last session highlighting positive comments and discuss anything that you think the group needs to process or give you further information on.

2.   Chapter 3 Learning Objectives (10 min.)

Introduce the chapter with a statement such as:

> **This chapter focuses on a variety of ways to practice the skills of self-empowerment. These skills help buffer the challenges of leadership and create opportunities for personal development.**

Read (or ask for volunteers to read) the *Chapter 3 Learning Objectives: Leadership and Self-Empowerment* slide (S1):

- Develop or clarify a personal vision for your work.

- Practice listening and communication skills that focus on "being present"

- Understand the qualities of mindful leadership

- Practice simple strategies for incorporating mindfulness into daily activities

- Assess the types of supports and stressors you experience in the workplace

- Create a good balance between your work and personal life.

- Develop and practice steps in a personal stress-reduction and wellness program.

3. "Some of the toughest things about being a leader" survey (15 min.)

Introduce this warm-up activity with a statement such as:

> It's not easy being a leader! Sometimes it seems like anything that could go wrong, does go wrong—and all in the same week! To help you appreciate that you're not alone, this activity is a survey to find out what you and others here might have in common as you reflect on some of the toughest things about being a supervisor or leader.

Distribute copies of the *Some of the toughest things about being a supervisor or leader* survey (H1). Ask the group to spend about 10 minutes circulating around the room and writing in names of other people who have experienced one or more of the situations listed. Encourage them to think of the activity as a way to "unload" these things, find common ground with other leaders, and then relax about them. After about 10 minutes, ask the group to reconvene.

Facilitate a brief discussion using this question:

In what ways can you focus on your own empowerment when events or circumstances such as these occur?

H1 Some of the toughest things about being a leader or supervisor

Find a leader or supervisor who has experienced:

1. Spending a lot of personal or staff time writing a grant proposal that didn't get funded _____

2. Trying to support a colleague or staff member with many personal or work-related problems _____

3. Being promoted and becoming a supervisor of staff members who used to be peers _____

4. Having to do a lot of work-related travel or taking work home at night or on weekends _____

5. Losing funding for a program and having to reassign or lay-off staff members _____

6. Not having adequate resources (money, equipment, staff, time, etc.) to implement an effective program_____

7. Having agency or program outcomes fail to meet projections or expectations due to factors beyond the agency's or program's control _____

8. Working as a supervisor or leader in an agency or program for less than a year _____

9. Managing staff members who have a lot of conflict with each other _____

10. Having to act as mediator or "go-between" when staff members and administrators have different views _____

11. Difficulty focusing on their agency's vision due to a major crisis or string of emergencies _____

12. Changes in their personal or family life as a result of being a supervisor or leader _____

4.   Recognizing your strengths as a supervisor and leader (30 min.)

Introduce this topic with the following question:

> **Can you name someone who exemplifies strong and effective leadership?**

Write participants' responses on easel paper. Then ask:

> **What strengths or qualities make (or made) them good leaders?**

Write the responses on the easel paper around the names from the previous question.

Distribute an index card to each participant. On one side of the card, ask them to write one of their strengths as a supervisor or leader. On the other side of the card, ask them to describe a situation in which they demonstrated that strength.

When the group is ready, ask them to turn to a person next to them and share the strength and situation with each other for a few minutes. After a few minutes, ask the group to reconvene. Ask if anyone would like to describe how it felt to share this information with a partner. Thank them for sharing their experience with the rest of the group. Then summarize:

> **As we think about self-empowerment and leadership, it's important to reflect on who and what has influenced our perceptions of effective leadership.**

Strength in Your Name[*]

Ask the leaders to take out a sheet of paper (or have some available) and write the first letter of both their first and last names vertically on the paper. Ask them to write a strength or positive characteristic that starts with each letter that is representative of who they are. Give a few examples if needed. After a few minutes, ask if anyone is willing to share the strengths in their name.

Conclude with the idea that it is sometimes difficult for leaders to recognize their own strengths, especially when feeling stressed or overwhelmed with responsibilities both at work and in their personal life. In this chapter, we'll be exploring a variety of ways to enhance their inner strengths and create a better work/life balance which can lead to increased self-empowerment.

[*] Thanks to New York City FDC Instructor Rosalyn Ferguson for suggesting this activity, which she uses in her classes.

5.   Clarifying a personal vision for your work (30 min.)

Introduce the topic and activity with a statement such as:

> As supervisors and leaders, you spend a lot of your time supporting the work of others—helping them develop steps to achieve goals. You contribute time to helping others realize their personal visions. Now it's time to focus on clarifying your personal vision for your work.

> This activity involves spending about 10 minutes talking with a partner about your personal vision for work right now and another 10 minutes writing a "Leadership Vision for Work" statement. You'll have a total of 20 minutes. You can decide when to finish talking to your partner and begin writing your personal vision statement.

Distribute copies of the *Clarifying a personal vision for your work* worksheet (H2). If possible, allow people to have more open space (move to a lobby, outside, or sit in other areas) to have time to talk and write their statement. (This is an opportunity for people to think, reflect, and share informally).

Set a predetermined return time for 20 minutes, allowing for extra time if needed. When the group reconvenes, ask for general reactions to questions on the worksheet. Ask if anyone would like to share their vision statement. If no one chooses to share their statement, move to facilitating a brief discussion using these questions:

1. How does it feel to talk with another leader about the reasons you entered family support work?

2. Writing a personal leadership vision statement for your work can be difficult. Why might it be hard to put these ideas on paper?

H2 Worksheet: Clarifying a personal vision for your work

Read each question and write down your ideas to share with a partner. Then use the ideas to write a personal vision statement for your work.

1.   Why did I go into this kind of work?

2.   What are the things I do in my work that makes my community and world a better place?

3.   What still needs to happen to make the work I do more effective?

4.   What skills, abilities and talents do I have that make a helpful difference in the lives of my staff members and colleagues?

5.   What would make my work more enjoyable and meaningful to me right now?

6.   What can I do today to transform my vision into a reality?

My Personal Vision for Work Statement

Based on your responses to the questions above, write a short statement that clarifies the vision you have for your work right now.

_____

_____

_____

_____

6.   Shifting your focus from "doing" to "being" (30 min.)

Introduce this topic and activity with a brief discussion using this question:

> How do you feel when you are with someone who gives you their undivided attention?

Thank participants for sharing. Then continue:

> To practice shifting our focus from "doing" to "being," we'll work in pairs for the next 10 minutes. For this activity, you need to talk with your partner about a very important day in your life—maybe it was a graduation, birthday, or other family event—or maybe it was something that happened in your work or an important personal accomplishment.
>
> Choose an event that you consider a high point in your life. When it's your turn, take five minutes to describe that event to your partner and include the thoughts and emotions you remember experiencing on that day.
>
> Talk with your partner about what led up to the event, who was there, when and where it happened, and include as many details as you can remember about how you felt at the time. Your partner's role is to listen with their full, undivided attention.
>
> Your partner should ask questions only if required to clarify what you've said. After five minutes, switch roles, and let the other person share their event while you provide undivided attention. After 10 minutes or so, we'll reconvene and have some discussion. Are there any questions?

After 10 minutes, allowing more time if needed, ask the group to reconvene. Facilitate a discussion using the following questions:

---

1.   How did it feel to have undivided attention while you were sharing your story? Were you able to share the story in a way that captured the essence of the experience for you?

2.   What did you do to give your undivided attention to your partner? What did you learn about yourself or your partner through this activity?

---

7.   Mindful leadership (30–45 min.)

Introduce this topic with a statement such as:

> The quality of being fully alert and aware is called mindfulness. In the study of creativity, mindfulness is sometimes called "flow." In athletics, it's sometimes called "being in the zone." Sometimes it's helpful to define a concept by the quality that it is not. Think of "mindfulness" as the opposite of "mindlessness." Mindfulness is not something you have to acquire—you already have it. Mindfulness is a practice that seeks to restore your natural capacity to be fully present in your life.

Review the *What is mindfulness?* slide (S2). Then continue:

> As a leader and supervisor, you have so much to do every day. You're probably thinking that, even if it were possible to be fully present in every task and with every person, you would still never be able to get everything done. Mindful leadership is not another management technique. It is an approach to supervision, leadership and life. Here are some of the benefits of supervising and leading with mindfulness:

Read (or ask for a volunteer to read) the *Benefits of mindful leadership* slide (S3).

There are several suggested video segments on mindfulness listed in the supplemental resources at the beginning of the chapter. We suggest reviewing these in advance and selecting one or more to share with the class. Or, choose another mindfulness related video of your choice.

Review the *Practical strategies for mindful leadership* slide (S4). Then facilitate discussion using the following question:

> **What other things do you do to give your undivided attention to a task or project?**

8.   Mindfulness exercises (30–45 min.)

Introduce this topic with an opening statement such as:

> There are many ways to cultivate mindfulness in our everyday exchanges and activities. This chapter suggests several simple exercises that can be an introduction to mindfulness practice. They include mindful breathing, mindful stretching, mindful walking and mindful listening. One of these exercises is called a "mindful minute" to help you get in touch with breathing, living and being fully aware for one minute.

Activity: "Mindful Minute"

> To practice being mindful for a minute, you already have everything you need to do it successfully. All you need is you. To start, you need to get as comfortable as you can.

Invite people to move their chairs to create more open space in the room. If people are dressed appropriately, suggest that they can sit on the floor or with their back against a wall. Make suggestions based on what you think is best.

> I'll guide you through the "mindful minute" so you don't need to think about time. You can close or cover your eyes, look out the window, or at something in the room that is soothing.

If you think it's helpful, dim the lights or close the blinds, depending on the environment. Have a watch with a second hand or use another device to time the minute if you want, but don't be overly concerned about timing it exactly. The whole point is to demonstrate how they can be mindful for very short periods of time as they are available during the day.

Read the following "Mindful Minute Guide" slowly with a soothing voice.

Mindful Minute Guide

> Let's begin our mindful minute. Find a comfortable sitting position. Allow your body to relax, drop your shoulders, and rest your arms and legs. Close or half-close your eyes, or if you prefer, keep them open and focus on a comforting sight.

Pause for about 5 to 10 seconds and let the room become still. Continue with:

> Start by listening to the sounds around you … the subtle sounds … like the sound of air moving around the room … soft sounds in the background … let your awareness go deeper to listen to the sound of your own breathing.

> Listen to the sound of your own breath going in and out … in your mind, see the air going in and see the air going out.

> If thoughts or emotions arise, notice them, but don't follow their story line. Instead, consider them as clouds drifting by on a summer day.

> Be aware of how your body is responding right now … be aware of the sensations of breathing in your chest, the gentle beating of your heart, the way that your back rests into the curve of the chair.

> **Be here in fullness of your being … your breathing, your heart beating, the clouds of your thoughts and emotions gently passing by.**

Pause for about 10 seconds to allow participants an opportunity to be immersed silently in this feeling. Then continue:

> **Listen to the sound of your breathing, aware of the air going in and out … listen to the sounds in the room … the subtle sounds around you. … When you feel comfortable, begin to open your eyes or refocus on your body, alert and aware.**

After this activity, don't try to process it immediately. Allow people to stand up, stretch, and slowly come back to the class experience. Gently, ask people how it felt.

Summarize by saying that a mindful minute is something you can do when stress starts building up wherever you happen to be.

There are also short podcasts that you can review in advance (see Supplemental Resources at the beginning of this chapter for suggestions) and select one or more to play for the group to create a "peaceful presence." If you choose more than one, you could also play them at other times during the class session.

Activity: "Peaceful Presence"*

Introduce this activity with a statement such as:

> In order to offer a compassionate presence to others, you first need to be able to reach a compassionate calm yourself. When you are deeply calm, chemicals called endorphins are released in your brain that send quieting messages through your body. You feel relaxed, calm, and may experience a greater sense of harmony between your body and mind—simply put, you may feel a "peaceful presence."

> Most times, you have a choice about how to respond to events in your life. You can push on with frenzy or respond by seeking a peaceful presence.

> Some leaders are physically present but spend much of their time solving and doing things for others that many times the staff members could do or solve for themselves. Leadership focused on offering empowering, compassionate support involves being fully present (physically, mentally, and emotionally) and offering your assistance when it's needed to help others develop healthy self-reliance.

> The first step in making this shift is to be fully present. As you listen to the podcast, pay attention to what you are feeling as you experience your own awareness of peaceful presence. After we're done listening, I'll invite anyone to share their ideas or feelings about the experience.

Invite participants to sit comfortably, to move chairs, or change places to get an outdoor view if there is one. When everyone is ready, play the podcast adjusting the sound for the best listening level. When the podcast ends, wait about 10 seconds before inviting the group to reconvene.

Facilitate a brief discussion using these questions:

1. Would anyone like to share how they are feeling right now?

2. Does anyone have an activity you do that helps you to relax and experience a sense of peaceful presence?

Participants who are uncomfortable with this type of activity may also share that the experience made them feel restless or bored. Accept whatever comments participants share, thanking them for their response as a genuine expression of their feeling or experience.

The goal of the activity is to help participants experience (and if they are willing), to share the feelings and sensations of a physically relaxed and mentally alert state. At the end of the activity, allow some time for light conversation as people come back to full participation before introducing the next activity.

* The concept and term "Peaceful Presence" was developed by Dr. Claire Forest.

9.   Removing distractions (30 min.)

Introduce the topic and activity with a statement such as:

> Distractions such as the chatty co-worker, or television have long been a challenge to focusing on work and family life, but today's highly technological world seems to bring a constant stream of e-mails, texts, tweets and other social media distractions that we feel compelled to check 24/7.

Ask participants:

> What are some of the most common distractions that keep you from focusing on what's most important?

If desired, write the responses on easel paper. Then continue:

> While technology is certainly not the only distraction we face, Dr. Kimberly Young is one of the first psychologists to document internet addiction and to characterize impulse control disorders related to various uses of technology.

Ask participants:

> How do you feel a leader's use of technology in the workplace might impact employees both positively and negatively?

Distribute the *Removing Distractions* worksheet (H3). Then continue:

> Working alone, take five minutes to list the primary distractions (of any type) in your own life that keep you from focusing on or doing what's most important to you. Be honest with yourself and as specific as possible.

After five minutes, ask each person to select the most distracting item on their list. Then find a partner and discuss with each other ideas for how they could minimize or remove it. In addition, challenge them to try it out for a specified period of time. Depending on what it is, the time frame could be one day, one week, one month, etc. Allowing enough time for their discussion, ask if anyone would like to share their distraction and solutions with the group.

Conclude by suggesting they check in with their partner at the next class session to report on their progress.

H3 Worksheet: Removing Distractions

List the most significant daily distractions that keep you from doing what's really important. You may have the same distraction under one or more of the categories.

Work related:

Personal:

Technological:

Steps I can take to remove or minimize the biggest distraction:
(Be specific, and indicate time frames whenever possible.)

For the next week, implement the steps you have listed, reflecting on how it went and if it helped you find more time for what is really important.

10.　Feeling good about the work you do (30 min.)

Introduce this topic and activity with a statement such as:

> Think about the people you work with- employees you supervise, your supervisor, co-workers and colleagues from other departments or agencies. Which of these people do you feel are highly supportive of you and your work? These are the people who trust that you are competent and are doing your best.

> A great way to take care of yourself and feel good about the work you do is to take time and appreciate those who do their best to support you at work. Here are a few ways to build up a network of people who will support you.

Review the *Feeling good about the work you do* slide (S5). Then continue:

> Think of someone in your workplace or community who you consider to be an ally or someone who has been especially supportive. It could also be someone who has been a mentor to you.

> Take the next five minutes and write this individual a short note of thanks for their help and support. It you want, give a specific example. It doesn't have to be long. Just say what's on your mind and from the heart.

Allow enough time for the group to finish their notes and ask if anyone is willing to share, if they are comfortable doing so. Encourage the group to give their letters to the individuals they wrote to during the next week.

Summarize with a brief discussion using these questions:

---

1. Have you ever received a note of thanks or other communication of thanks from a staff member or colleague you've worked with? If so, how did it feel to be appreciated?

2. How often do you express your appreciation to those you supervise?

---

11.   The Family Circles Assessment adapted for leaders (30 min.)

Introduce this activity with a statement such as:

> One of the most important ways to feel good about the work you do is to have a healthy support system in your life. Having supportive relationships is more than just having a close friend and colleague to talk with when you need it. Here's an analogy to remind you how important it is to take care of yourself by taking care of the important relationships in your life.

> Tomorrow when you go to your office, look around for any green or flowering plants. (If you don't have a plant near your desk, look at the common areas whether inside or outside the building). How do those plants look? Are they healthy and blooming? Or are they looking like they haven't been watered for weeks? Plants are like support systems. If you get busy and forget about them, they can hold on for a while; but if you neglect them too long, they just die. And if you fuss with them too much—picking and pruning all the time or watering too often—you can kill them with kindness.

> Support systems are like plants, in a way, because they are always changing, even if you can't see the changes. One day, you might look at a plant and see a shoot appear. A few days later, a bud appears. Then one day to your surprise, a bloom is there. Support systems are like plants, living and growing all the time.

> The Family Circles Assessment for Leaders is an adaptation of the one used in FDC training to help workers identify the stressors and supports in their lives. For this activity, I'll guide you through the seven circles of the form and ask you to write in the names and the qualities of people in your life right now.

Refer to the blank *Family Circles Assessment adapted for leaders* in their book. or distribute copies of the *Family Circles Assessment adapted for leaders* worksheet (H4). Read the directions for completing each circle from the *Family Circles Assessment adapted for leaders guide* (H5), keeping an even pace but allowing enough time, so that the group can be thoughtful as they fill in the circles. After you've guided them through the circles, give them another minute to go back and finish up.

Tell participants:

> You've completed filling in the circles with the names and the qualities of people in your support system. Great. Now, hold the page out in front of you and look at it again blurring the individual words. Look at where your writing appears on the page. Are some circles full of writing and others empty or near empty?

> Let's do one more thing to help you understand another aspect of your supports. Look over the things you've written and do two things: draw a circle around the things you've written that are supportive. Then, go back and draw a box around the things on the assessment that are stressful for you. Anything you've written can have a circle, a box, or both if it is a support and a stressor.

Give people a few minutes to finish with this part of the activity and then facilitate a brief discussion using these questions:

1. Based on completing this self-assessment, what have you learned about your current support system?

2. If you want to increase the supports you have in any area what would you do?

H4 The Family Circles Assessment adapted for leaders

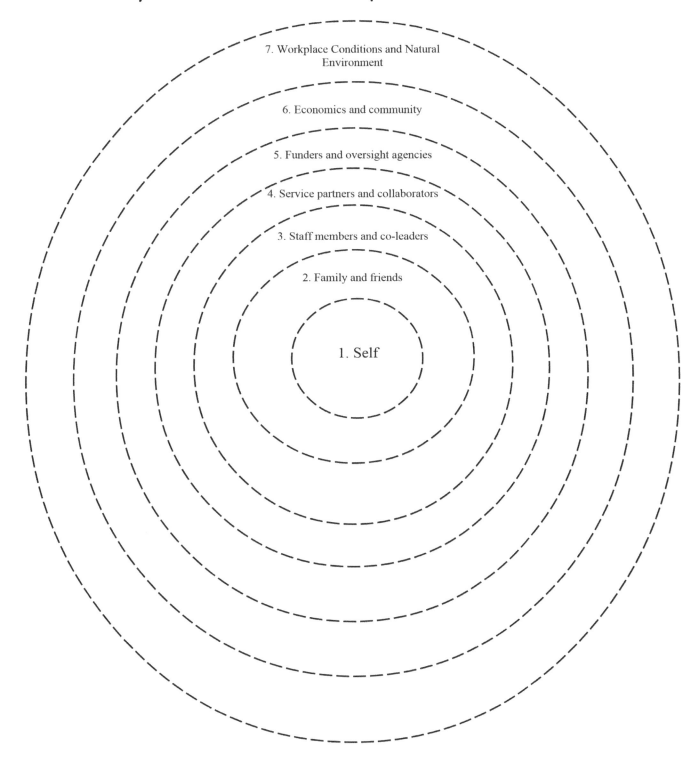

7. Workplace Conditions and Natural Environment

6. Economics and community

5. Funders and oversight agencies

4. Service partners and collaborators

3. Staff members and co-leaders

2. Family and friends

1. Self

Note: The lines between the circles are dotted to show they are fluid. You decide where to list someone.

H5 The Family Circles Assessment adapted for leaders guide

The lines are dashed to show they are fluid—you decide where to list someone. You might even decide to ignore lines or modify category names to make the model work best for you.

1. *Yourself*: You are at the center of your world, List your guiding principles about leadership and your personal vision for your work. Note your strengths and dreams, and the goals you wish to achieve as a leader. Note any qualities or conditions that influence your leadership.

2. *Family members and friends*: List the names of your partner (if you have one), family members, and friends (including extended family or informal networks). Note their qualities or aspects of the relationship that mean a lot to you and how these relationships influence your leadership.

3. *Staff members, your supervisor, coleaders, or board*: List names of those with whom you communicate on a daily basis. You can also include the names of individuals who you feel significantly contribute to you and your agency's overall well-being (e.g. professional colleagues, volunteers, community supporters and key advisors). Note the ways they influence you and your agency.

4. *Service partners and collaborators*: List the names of individuals or agencies that work with your agency in providing family support in your community. Note the ways they influence you or your agency. You can also identify your agency's professional associations, interagency networks, and state and national affiliations.

5. *Funders and oversight agencies*: List the primary funders for your program or agency and, if different, the names of departments that oversee and monitor programs and agency outcomes. Note the ways they influence you and your agency.

6. *Economics and community*: Note the social, political and economic influences that currently affect your role as a leader in your organization (e.g. state and local policies, poverty, employment levels in your community). Describe your community and how it affects your workplace. Note how local, state, national and global trends are affecting you as a leader (e.g. hiring freezes, budget cuts and unionization).

7. *Workplace conditions and natural environment*: Note how the conditions of the workplace and natural environment affect you and other leaders in your agency (e.g. easy or difficult commute to work, travel required to programs at different locations, a nearby park for walks during lunch breaks, level of safety for workers on home visits).

12. Balancing work and personal life (30 min.)

Introduce this topic and activity with a statement such as:

> Keeping your work and personal life in balance can be difficult. A satisfying personal life can help keep frustrations at work in perspective, and a fulfilling job can help you cope with the ups and downs of family life and responsibilities outside of work.

These are suggestions from the chapter to consider:

Review the *Ways to balance work and personal life* slide (S6). Distribute copies of the *Balancing your work and personal life* worksheet (H6). Continue with:

> Here's a worksheet to help you assess what's going well in your life right now and what you wish you could change. Write your ideas in each of the corresponding triangles. Then, go on to the part below. Under the list of things going well, write the strengths and supports you get from these things in your life. Then, under the list of things you wish you could change, write ideas for ways you could ask others to help you. After you've finished, find a partner and take turns sharing what you wrote.

After about 15 minutes, ask the group to reconvene. Lead a discussion using these questions:

---

1. What are some other ways you have learned to balance your work and personal life?

2. How do employees benefit when supervisors find a healthy balance between their work and personal lives?

3. What are some ways supervisors can support their staff in creating a healthy work/life balance?

H6 Worksheet: Balancing your work and family life

Directions: List the corresponding items in each triangle. In the space below, list strengths and supports you get from what's going well, and ways that others could help you change the things you can.

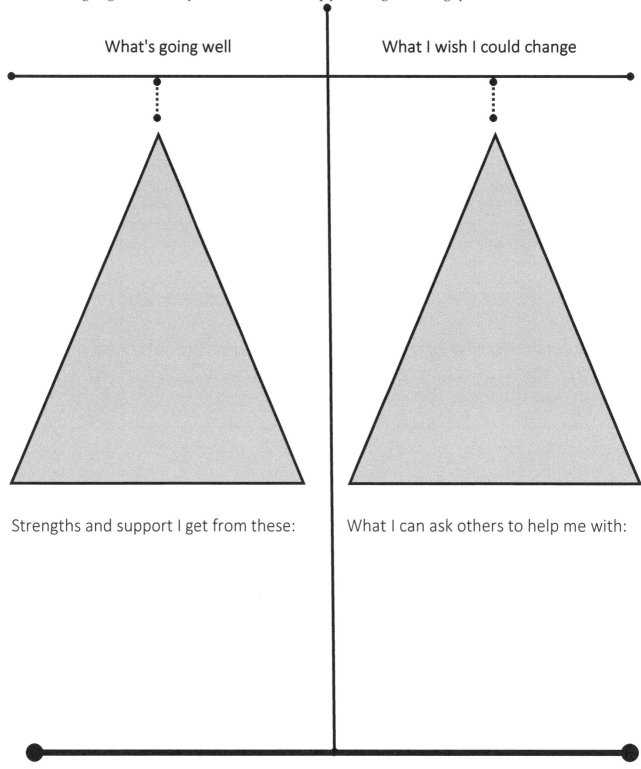

What's going well

What I wish I could change

Strengths and support I get from these:

What I can ask others to help me with:

13. Creating your own stress-reduction and wellness program (30 min.)

Introduce this topic and activity with a statement such as:

> Stress is a reality in our lives and can have a detrimental impact on our health and well-being, but there are ways we can reduce its negative effects.

Review the *Effects of chronic stress on health and well-being* slide (S7).

> The following analogy describes the balance between positive and negative stress.

Read (or ask for a volunteer to read) the *A Potter's View of Stress* slide (S8). Facilitate a brief discussion with these questions:

> 1. If you imagine the potter in this passage as a leader and the pottery as a family-serving organization, how does a leader determine the amount of pressure or stress needed to lead the organization effectively?
>
> 2. What events or situations occur in an organization that resemble the pottery's "firing" and require a period of rest before and after?

Tell participants:

> Here is a list of ways that supervisors and leaders can reduce stress and increase overall health and wellness:

Read (or ask for volunteers to read) the *Components of a personal stress reduction and wellness program* slide (S9).

> Maybe you have already incorporated some of these elements of stress reduction and wellness in your life. If you have, that's great. If you haven't or if you'd like to do more, this activity is a chance to develop a plan to introduce some of these ideas over the next month.

Distribute copies of the *Stress Reduction and Wellness calendar* (H7), or give them the option of using an electronic calendar. Ask people to write today's date on the corresponding day in the first week of the calendar, and number the days of the calendar to end at one month from today. Then continue:

> Use this calendar to help yourself become more mindful about ways you can reduce stress and increase your health and wellness over the next month. For each week, write a few things that you could try to do. You don't need to write in something for every day. Try to put in a variety of ideas each week. Take 5 or 10 minutes to develop your plan and then share your plan with a partner who will provide you with supportive feedback.

After about 5–10 minutes (more if the group needs), ask them to share their plan with a partner. Reinforce this is a way to help them stay mindful of reducing stress and promoting wellness in their lives. Suggest they keep the calendar close at hand for the next month. This could also be their Independent Learning Project for Chapter 3, if they wish. Mention that at the next session, you'll ask for any volunteers to share their progress.

H7 Stress-reduction and wellness calendar

Month .... **Year** ....

	Sunday	Monday	Tuesday	Wednesday	Thursday	Friday	Saturday

14. Planning an Independent Learning Project and the Leadership Empowerment Plan (30 min.)

By the end of Chapter 3, participants should be thinking about what their Leadership Empowerment Plan might look like. This is a good time to review the form and respond to any questions. Reinforce that this is a great opportunity to apply the concepts and competencies learned to a relevant workplace project.

Although the project does not have to be completed by the end of the course, ideally, they would begin implementing their plan, so there is ample time to project out a thirty- day update and reflection on their progress by the end of the last class session. In addition, invite them to spend a few minutes thinking about their Independent Learning Project for Chapter 3, which is intended to demonstrate what they have learned.

Allow time for meeting with their Peer Advisors to discuss and develop a project for Chapter 3 along with the empowerment plan. Remind them the Peer Advisor's role is to support each other in brainstorming and creating a manageable plan and time frame to complete their projects.

Leadership Empowerment Plan for _____

Today's date: _____

Short-term goal:

_____

Steps leading to this goal

Steps you will take and when: *Steps your peer advisor will take and when*:

_____   _____

_____   _____

_____   _____

Your personal assets and strengths

In your words: *In your peer advisor's words*:

_____   _____

_____   _____

_____   _____

Concerns

In your words: *In your peer advisor's words*:

_____   _____

_____   _____

_____   _____

Services and resources available: (include names, addresses, phone numbers, etc.)

_____

Date, time, and place to review progress: _____

I will support _____'s plan to achieve this goal and agree to meet to review progress.

_____

Peer advisor's signature   Date

15.   Quick Feedback Form (10 min.)

Distribute copies of the feedback form at the end of the session for leaders to complete before they leave.

Empowerment Skills for Leaders

Chapter 3: Leadership and Self-Empowerment

Quick Feedback Form

When during the session did you feel most engaged?

When during the session did you feel least engaged?

What would make your experience in this course better?

Thanks for your feedback!

Chapter 3 PowerPoint slides

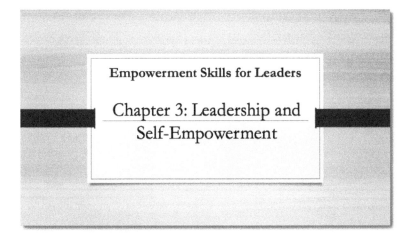

Empowerment Skills for Leaders

Chapter 3: Leadership and Self-Empowerment

Chapter 3: Learning Objectives

* Develop or clarify a personal leadership vision for your work.
* Practice listening and communication skills that focus on "being present".
* Understand the qualities of mindful leadership.
* Practice simple strategies for incorporating mindfulness in daily activities.
* Assess the types of supports and stressors you experience in the workplace.
* Create a good balance between your work and personal life.
* Develop and practice steps in a personal stress reduction and wellness program.

S1

What is mindfulness?

Mindfulness is not a technique, rather it is an approach to your work and life. A practice that seeks to restore your natural capacity to be fully present in your leadership, supervision and life. And, the benefits are great…

S2

Benefits of mindful leadership

Creates an opportunity for you to:

❖ Appreciate the creative ways that working with others can expand your perspective and increase your capacity to find new and innovative solutions.

❖ Bring all of "who you are" as a unique individual to your work.

❖ Realign your leadership style with your leadership vision in order to empower yourself and others.

S3

Benefits of mindfulness (continued)

❖ Reframe the limited view of leadership based on "command and control" into a vision of leadership through empowerment and transformation.

❖ Allows you to go beyond conditioned responses.

❖ Increased productivity

❖ Better relationships

❖ Lower stress

S3

Practical strategies for mindful leadership

* Spend your time on what is important
* Set realistic goals for your work and personal life
* Schedule your most important work during the time of day you feel most productive
* Delegate
* Communicate efficiently
* Carve out time for quiet reflection and mindfulness practice

S4

Feeling good about the work you do

* Practice healthy ways to express your feelings- skillfully managing conflict can help people understand and become open to other's points of view.
* Have some fun- nurtures creativity and provides significant health benefits.
* Look for opportunities in challenges- people with optimistic attitudes tend to cope more effectively with stress.
* Treat yourself with compassion and care- you'll have renewed energy to decide what's important and follow through.
* Establish appropriate boundaries with staff and colleagues- you can build genuine, honest and caring relationships while safeguarding your privacy and theirs.

S5

Ways to balance work and personal life

➤ Take a personal inventory of what is working well in your work and personal life right now, "count your blessings" and your strengths.

➤ Note the things you wish you could change.

➤ Ask family members to share the workload at home and delegate more at work.

➤ Ask for help when needed.

➤ Consider communicating your challenges within the organization.

➤ Practice mindfulness

S6

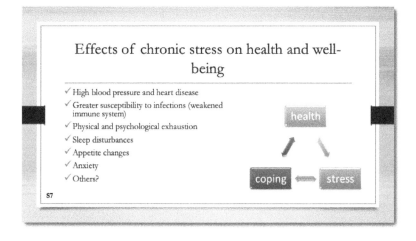

Effects of chronic stress on health and well-being

✓ High blood pressure and heart disease
✓ Greater susceptibility to infections (weakened immune system)
✓ Physical and psychological exhaustion
✓ Sleep disturbances
✓ Appetite changes
✓ Anxiety
✓ Others?

S7

The Potter's View of Stress

As a potter presses clay on a spinning wheel, a shape begins to emerge. The rotation of the pottery wheel and the gentle, yet firm hand of the potter work together to mold a mass of clay into a beautiful form.

If the potter exerts too much pressure, the clay will break or tear. If the potter exerts too little pressure, the clay will not transform into a piece of pottery

S8

Potter's View of Stress (continued)

After the potter is done making the pot, the clay must "rest" before being fired.

Like clay pots, we can become our best when we experience enough stress, but not too much. We also need time to rest, especially before and after times of "fire" in our lives.

S8

Components of a stress reduction and wellness program

- Daily mindfulness practice
- Exercise you enjoy enough to actually do
- Healthy foods that you like enough to actually eat
- Friends and family who care about you (and you about them)
- Letting go of harmful habits
- Having some fun
- Counseling
- Others?

S9

CHAPTER 4
SUPERVISING WITH SKILL AND HEART

Teaching materials

- LCD projector/smart board and power points

- Easel, easel paper, and markers

- Masking or cellophane tape

- Copies of handouts and materials

- Melodic bell or chime (for reconvening the group)

- Supplementary resources (optional)

- Refreshments (optional)

	Activities	Approximate Duration (minutes)	Slides	Handouts/Materials
1	*Agenda and Ch. 3 Feedback Summary*	5		
2	*Ch. 4 Learning Objectives*	10	S1 Learning objectives for Ch. 4	
3	*Staying focused on the "vision" of supervision*	20	S2 About Perception	
4	*Developing bifocal and peripheral vision*	30	S3 Bifocal and peripheral vision S4 A worker's office line drawing S5 Tunnel vision	H1 A worker's office line drawing
5	*Developing mutually respectful relationships*	15	S6 Guidelines to help you decide what to share	
6	*Guidelines for strengths-based assessment*	30–45	S7 Guidelines for using strengths-based assessment S8 Incorporating five key areas into your performance review process	H2 Sample Employee Performance Review Form
7	*Supporting staff through major transitions*	30	S9 Situations in which employees may experience grief/loss S10 Typical stages of grief S11 Ways to help staff during major transitions	H3 Grief/loss case situations
8	*Helping staff members manage workplace stress and burnout*	45	S12 Potential factors contributing to job burnout S13 Symptoms of job burnout	H4 Yolanda's Story H5 Steps of family development adapted for a supervisor-worker relationship
9	*Handling trauma in the workplace*	30–45	S14 Situations that may create risk of traumatic stress S15 Symptoms of post-traumatic stress S16 Examples of reframing responses	
10	*Resolving conflict*	30	S17 Submission-aggression loop in a supervisor–staff member relationship	H6 Principles and practices of family development compared with principal negotiation H7 Resolving-conflict case studies

Activities	Approximate Duration (minutes)	Slides	Handouts/Materials
11 *Handling blame, criticism and difficulties with your supervisor*	30	S18 Basic format of an "I" message S19 Responses to an "I" message	H8 "I" message situation cards
12 *Group dynamics in the workplace*	30	S20 Developmental stages of a group S21 Suggestions to successfully manage dynamics of group development	
13 *Reflecting-in-action and single- and double-loop learning*	30	S22 Single- and double-loop learning in organizations	H9 Worksheet: Single- and double-loop learning in organizations H10 Reflecting-in-action and single- and double-loop learning case situations
14 *Facilitating effective staff meetings and in-service training programs*	30	S23 Techniques to facilitate creative small group discussion	
15 *Planning for Leadership Empowerment Plans and Cultural Luncheon*	10		
16 *Planning Independent Learning Projects*	30		
17 *Participant Feedback Forms*	10		Quick Feedback Form

Supplemental Resources

There are resources at the end of each chapter in the *Empowerment Skills for Leaders* Handbook. A suggestion would be to select one of the articles listed (or another of your choice) that you feel is relevant and of interest to the group and distribute copies for them to read (or refer them to a link online) before the next class session. At the beginning of the next class session, facilitate a brief discussion about the article and how it reinforces the concepts covered in the chapter.

Links to additional resources are on the FDC website, www.familydevelopmentcredential.org, under Instructor Resources.

Publications

Goddard, H. Wallace, and James P. Marshall. "Getting Our Hearts Right: Three Keys to Better Relationships." University of Arkansas Cooperative Extension Service. https://www.uaex.edu/life-skills wellness/personal-family-well-being/personal/getting-hearts-right.aspx.

Russo, Eileen M. *What's My Communication Style? 3rd Edition Facilitator Guide.* Training and Development Materials of Canada. http://www.olresources.ca/product/view/whats-my-communication-style-3rd-edition-facilitator-guide.

Vavrichek, Sherrie M. *The Guide to Compassionate Assertiveness: How to Express Your Needs and Deal with Conflict While Keeping a Kind Heart.* Oakland, CA: New Harbinger, 2012.

Videos

YouTube. "Change Blindness" videos. There are a variety to choose from.

Activities

1.   Agenda and feedback summary (10 min.)

Provide a short summary of feedback from the last session highlighting positive comments and discuss any feedback that you think the group needs to process or give you further information on.

Give a brief overview of the day's agenda along with any needed logistics.

2.   Chapter 4 Learning objectives (5 min.)

Read (or ask for volunteers to read) the *Chapter 4 Learning objectives: Supervising with Skill and Heart* slide (S1):

- Use "peripheral vision" to see the strengths in staff members to better establish and build mutually respectful relationships.

- Expand your vision to see the "bigger picture" in goal setting and strategic planning.

- Determine how much personal information to share with staff members.

- Understand how to support staff during major organizational transitions.

- Increase awareness and help staff manage workplace stress and job burnout.

- Seek support in helping staff cope with traumatic events.

- Practice conflict resolution skills using the principles and practices of family development.

- Understand the dynamics of group development in the workplace.

- Use creative discussion techniques in staff meetings and with other groups.

3.   Staying focused on the "vision" of supervision warmup activity* (20 min.)

Begin the warm-up activity with the *About Perception* slide (S2). Ask participants:

What do you see?

After the group responds, continue:

You may have seen this picture before, but it is a good illustration of how people can look at the exact same thing and have different perceptions of what it is.

Show the "Change Blindness" video segment, or another one of your choice. Summarize by asking:

Why do our perceptions matter as we think about building authentic and effective relationships with our employees and colleagues?

---

* Thanks to FDC instructor Angela Zimmerman from Molloy College, Long Island, NY for suggesting this activity.

4.   Developing Bifocal and Peripheral Vision (30 min.)

Introduce this topic with a statement such as:

> In our context, "bifocal vision" is the ability to see on two levels at the same time. By using bifocal vision, you can see the reality of someone's current situation and at the same time see their natural strengths and resources.
>
> Another way to identify strengths in your staff members is to use "peripheral vision," the ability to observe and find similarities and common ground with those you supervise. One way to practice peripheral vision is to walk through your agency's office space as if you were a visitor and observe workspaces noticing photographs, posters, and other personal items. These "artifacts" can provide valuable clues to finding common ground with those you supervise.

Review the *Bifocal and Peripheral vision* slide (S3).

Project the *A worker's office line drawing* slide (S4) and distribute copies of it (H1) to the group. Ask participants to work with a partner and using their bifocal vision, generate a list of strengths they see in the drawing. After about five minutes, call time, and ask them to use their peripheral vision and generate a list of the similarities and areas of common interest they might have with this worker, based on what they see in the drawing.

Process the activity by first having each pair name a strength and see how many different ones they come up with. Follow by doing the same thing with the commonalities. If your group is small, another way to divide the group is to have them count off by two's. Have one group use bifocal vision and list the strengths and the other use peripheral vision and list the commonalities. Ask for a spokesperson from each group to present their ideas.

Facilitate a brief discussion using these questions:

1. How does "bifocal and peripheral vision" affect a supervisor's ability to see the reality of an employee's situation while, at the same time, recognizing the employee's strengths?

2. Can anyone think of a situation in which the ability to recognize an employee's strengths or something you had in common with them helped to keep some difficulty or problem in perspective?

3. How could a leader's "bifocal" and "peripheral" vision be useful in an interagency collaboration?

Conclude with:

> A third type of vision that can be problematic for leaders is "tunnel vision": the inability to see the bigger picture because too much attention is focused on extraneous or unimportant details.

Review the *Tunnel Vision* slide (S5).

> Correcting tunnel vision can be especially difficult because it's often used unconsciously. Reflecting-in-action is a technique that can help supervisors and leaders avoid tunnel vision. Later in this chapter, we'll be practicing this technique as it relates to agency goal setting and strategic planning.

H1 A worker's office

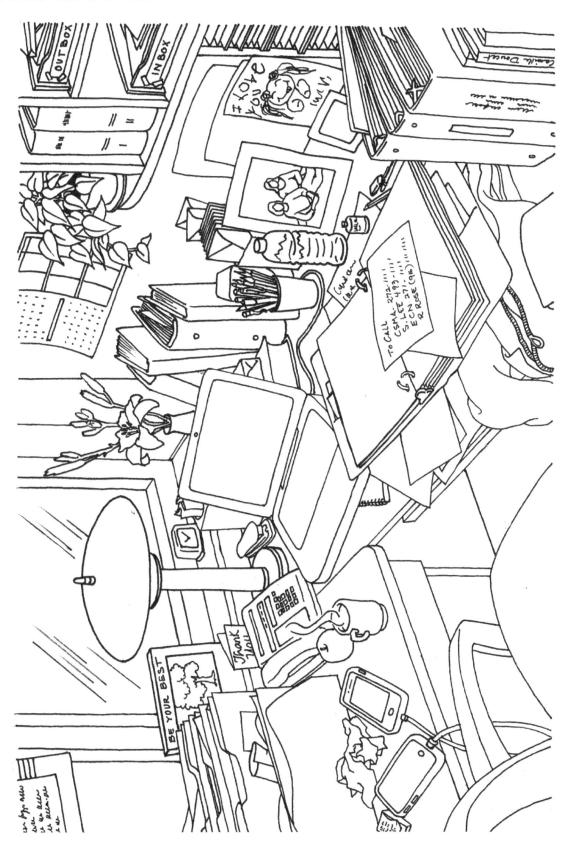

5.   Developing mutually respectful relationships (15 min.)

Introduce this topic with a statement such as this:

> When both leaders and staff members participate in empowerment-based trainings such as FDC, and they learn how to communicate more skillfully through listening well, paraphrasing, feedback, and "I" messages, the entire organization experiences positive outcomes.
>
> Developing mutually respectful relationships incorporates a healthy balance between listening to and sharing with each other. Some workers may share a lot of personal information and think that the relationship is one-sided unless you share personal information as well. So, how much of your own personal life should you share with staff members? Here are some guidelines to help you answer this question:

Read (or ask for volunteers to read) the *Guidelines to help you decide what to share* slide (S6). Then facilitate a brief discussion using these questions:

1. What are benefits of sharing aspects of your personal life with staff members?

2. As a supervisor and leader, what positive things do you learn about staff members when they are willing to share personal information?

6.   Guidelines for strengths-based assessment (30–45 min.)

Introduce this activity with a statement such as:

> Supervising with skill and heart requires that supervisors evaluate the efforts and competencies of staff members and teams using strengths-based assessment. Some agencies are required to use standardized forms for employee assessments, such as annual performance reviews. Some agencies also include individualized sections or design their own assessment forms. Here are some guidelines for using strengths-based assessment with staff members and teams:

Read (or ask volunteers to read) the *Guidelines for using strengths-based assessment* slide (S7). Distribute copies of the *Sample Employee Performance Review form* handout (H2).

> Here is a sample form that supervisors might use to assess a staff member's performance. We'll divide into groups of four and based on the guidelines we just read, revise or redesign the form to make it more strengths based. Each group will get a sheet of easel paper to revise the form or generate a list of ways to use this form in a strengths-based way. Work on this for about 10–15 minutes and then we'll reconvene. Please designate a spokesperson from your group to share your ideas with the larger group.

Arrange the group into small groups of 4 and give each group a sheet of paper and marker. Circulate during the activity to provide encouragement and answer questions. After about 10–15 minutes, ask each group's spokesperson to present their ideas. Then continue:

> The Corporate Leadership Council (United Kingdom 2010) conducted a survey of more than 19,000 staff members and found that a strengths-based management approach resulted in a 36% increase in performance as compared to a 27% decrease in performance associated with deficit-focused management.

Review the *Strengths-based employee assessment* slide (S8). Conclude with a brief discussion by asking:

> Based on the guidelines and this activity, how could your agency improve upon using a strengths-based approach to assess performance?

H2 Sample Employee Performance Review Form

Employee Name: _____

Agency: _____   Position: _____

Employment start date: _____   Date of review: _____

Circle the number indicating the current level of employee performance in the following areas:

		Always	Mostly	Usually	Sometimes	Rarely
1	*Organizes time and priorities to accomplish work tasks*	1	2	3	4	5
2	*Communicates effectively with families, colleagues, and supervisors*	1	2	3	4	5
3	*Submits work assignments in a timely and complete fashion*	1	2	3	4	5
4	*Demonstrates skills and competencies required to complete work assignments*	1	2	3	4	5
5	*Represents the agency in a professional manner*	1	2	3	4	5
6	*Seeks supervisor's support and feedback when appropriate*	1	2	3	4	5
7	*Follows agency's policies and procedures when using benefit time, equipment, and other agency resources*	1	2	3	4	5
8	*Fulfills responsibilities by attending continuing education and mandatory in-service trainings*	1	2	3	4	5

Supervisor's recommendation or comment:

_____

_____

_____

_____   _____
Supervisor's signature and date   Employee's signature and date

7.   Supporting staff through major transitions (30 min.)

Introduce this topic and activity with a statement such as:

> All organizations experience change over time, but some changes, such as layoffs and job cuts, affect staff morale and productivity in dramatic ways. When any person experiences a significant loss, such as losing their job or the death of a loved one, grief is a natural and normal response. Most people grieve over a period of time and through a series of stages. There are situations however, in which a person may feel unable to grieve or to ask for the support they need. Here are some situations in which employees may experience grief/loss in an organizational context:

Read (or ask for volunteers to read) the *Situations in which employees may experience grief/loss* slide (S9). Ask if anyone who has experienced any of these situations is willing to share how it affected them. Thank those who shared.

> The patience and responsiveness of supervisors who understand the grieving process can go a long way toward supporting staff members during these difficult times. Here are typical stages of the grieving process.

Read the *Typical stages of grief* slide (S10).

> In Chapter 1, we read a case study describing a major organizational change brought about by a funding cut in a well-established program. Let's review that case again, only this time focusing on how staff members might experience these four stages of grief. Let's generate a list of possible grief responses and then come up with ways in which a supervisor could support staff members during this transition.

Distribute the *Grief/loss case situations* handout (H3). Ask the group for their suggestions regarding each of the situations. Another option would be to divide the large group into small groups and assign each small group one of the situations, asking for a spokesperson to process.

Summarize by reviewing the *Supporting employees during major transitions* slide (S11). Then facilitate a brief discussion using the following question:

> **What factors might affect how individual staff members react to a major transition in your agency?**

H3 Grief/loss case situations

Situation 1

Funding for a well-established family support program in your organization has been unexpectedly cut due to a change in the political priorities in your community. This loss of funding will result in the need to lay off some newly hired workers who have brought much-needed creativity and cultural diversity to your organization. You need to decide how best to approach the situation, while striving to keep staff members' morale and productivity stable during the transition.

Situation 2

Your organization is in the process of restructuring departments and senior management responsibilities as a result of new funding or legislative requirements. You have been reassigned as the director of a new department. You know very little about the department because the former director left the organization without an explanation. You need to consider how you want to begin or re-establish relationships with supervisors and workers in this new capacity.

8.   Helping staff members manage workplace stress and "burnout" (45 min.)

Introduce this topic with a statement such as:

> Job burnout can occur in any job but the everyday stresses of supporting families at their most vulnerable times can be emotionally draining for family workers and staff members. In addition, staff members may be struggling to balance the demands of work and family resulting in emotional and physical distress that can lead to burnout. Here are some potential contributing factors that may put staff members at risk for experiencing burnout:

Review (or ask a volunteer to read) the *Potential contributors to job burnout* slide (S12). Tell participants:

> As a supervisor, it is important to recognize the symptoms of burnout so you can support staff members as needed.

Review the *Symptoms of job "burnout"* slide (S13). Continue with:

> "Yolanda's story" represents a hypothetical example of a family worker who appears at risk for job burnout. Let's read over the situation:

Distribute the *Yolanda's Story* handout (H4) and the *Steps of family development adapted for a supervisor-worker relationship* worksheet (H5) (the *Instructor Copy* is for your reference and has potential responses listed).

Ask for a volunteer(s) to read the story. Continue with:

> A supervisor could use the Steps of Family Development adapted for a supervisor-worker relationship to support Yolanda in handling or changing her current situation. Remember that these steps are a guide; not all steps will occur in every relationship, nor will they necessarily occur in this exact order.

> To practice using the steps of family development, choose a partner and identify three of the steps in the family development guide that a supervisor could use to support Yolanda. Then, together write statements illustrating the supervisor's response to Yolanda for each step. After about ten minutes, we'll reconvene and go through the seven steps. I'll ask for volunteers to share some of their responses.

After 10 minutes, or sooner if the group finishes, reconvene the group. Ask for volunteers to offer responses for each of the seven steps.

Facilitate a brief discussion using these questions:

1. Has anyone had a similar situation with a staff member?

2. How do you feel about using these steps to support a staff member when a personal difficulty isn't interfering with their job performance?

H4 Yolanda's story

Yolanda, a family worker you have supervised for the past two years, has asked to speak to you regarding a personal matter. During the time you have supervised her, she has been a dedicated and effective worker who has pleasant working relationships with her families, co-workers and other staff members.

When Yolanda comes in to see you, you suspect that she's been crying. When you ask her what she'd like to talk about, she describes some long-standing family problems that she hasn't shared with anyone else. She needs to move out of her current living situation, but she doesn't believe that she has the income or other supports to help her relocate. She thinks she would need to work a second job to afford an apartment of her own. She has a school-aged daughter, and she fears that the cost of childcare will consume whatever extra money she might make in a second job.

From what you know, Yolanda hasn't taken much time off and her work assignments are up to date. You had even been thinking about asking her to take on a special short-term assignment because she appeared so well organized. As a result of this meeting, you are worried about whether she'll even continue in her job with your agency.

Yolanda doesn't want anyone in the agency to know about her situation. You realize that the difficulties she's having are not primarily work-related, nor are they overtly affecting her job performance. But you feel that if you don't do something, the problems will eventually have an impact upon her work. You want to be helpful, but aren't sure what to do to be supportive, while still maintaining a professional presence and tone in the relationship.

Steps of family development adapted for a supervisor-worker relationship—Instructor Copy

Steps of Family Development adapted for a supervisor-worker relationship	Ways a supervisor can support Yolanda using a family development approach
1 *A supervisor develops a partnership with a worker.*	Listen well and empathically using basic communication skills such paraphrasing, feedback. Put her at ease with attentive nonverbal body language.
2 *A supervisor helps the worker assess their needs and strengths. This is an ongoing process.*	Share the strengths you have seen in her as a person and in her relationships with co-workers, collaborators, and families.
3 *A supervisor and worker set goals together and collaboratively identify ideas for achieving them.*	Assist her in thinking about and identifying a major goal she'd like to achieve. Help her brainstorm the steps she needs to take in order to achieve her goal.
4 *A supervisor helps a worker make a plan to achieve the goals with some of the tasks being the responsibility of the worker and some being the responsibility of the supervisor.*	Help her decide what steps she can take on her own and what steps you can help with.
5 *The supervisor and worker learn and practice skills needed to be inter-reliant. This is an ongoing process.*	Offer to meet again and, if she agrees, set a date and time to review progress and to plan the next step.
6 *The supervisor and worker collaborate using services as stepping-stones to help reach goals.*	Decide together what services, programs and contact information she needs to begin the first steps. Offer to help with getting names and phone numbers of agencies.
7 *A healthy balance between the supervisor's and worker's sense of responsibility is restored. The organization is strengthened through the process and the supervisor and worker are better able to handle future challenges.*	Consider ways that you, as her supervisor, can support the steps she has planned (i.e. flex time, vacation, personal days). Anticipate coverage for her essential work tasks during her time off. Think about ways she could be eligible for career advancement in the future.

H5 Worksheet: Steps of family development adapted for a supervisor-worker relationship

Steps of Family Development adapted for a supervisor-worker relationship	Ways a supervisor can offer support using a family development approach
1 *A supervisor develops a partnership with a worker.*	
2 *A supervisor helps the worker assess their needs and strengths. This is an ongoing process.*	
3 *A supervisor and worker set goals together and collaboratively identify ideas for achieving them.*	
4 *A supervisor helps a worker make a plan to achieve the goals with some of the tasks being the responsibility of the worker and some being the responsibility of the supervisor.*	
5 *The supervisor and worker learn and practice skills needed to be inter-reliant. This is an ongoing process.*	
6 *The supervisor and worker collaborate using services as stepping-stones to help reach goals.*	
7 *A healthy balance between the supervisor's and worker's sense of responsibility is restored. The organization is strengthened through the process and the supervisor and worker are better able to handle future challenges.*	

9.   Handling trauma in the workplace (30–45 min.)

Introduce this topic with a statement such as:

> Even workers who feel they have become desensitized to the plight of some families, can be shocked when one of their families experiences a catastrophe or traumatic event. Observing or witnessing the pain, suffering and trauma of others can result in an individual experiencing "vicarious trauma." Family workers who are habitually exposed to families' chronic hardships can begin to feel powerless and traumatized, especially if a shocking tragedy occurs.
>
> There are also instances in which a traumatic event of such intensity and magnitude occurs that workers, teams, an entire agency, or a community can be traumatized. Here are some situations in which the risk for traumatic stress exists:

Read the *Situations that may create risk for traumatic stress* slide (S14).

> Traumatic stress can overwhelm a person's natural coping skills and disrupt their ability to think, feel, and act in healthy ways. Medical treatment, counseling and the use of stress reduction techniques can be helpful to individuals coping with traumatic stress. Traumatic stress that remains untreated can put a person at risk for post-traumatic stress. Here are some symptoms that may indicate that a person is experiencing post-traumatic stress.

Read the *Symptoms of post-traumatic stress* slide (S15).

> As a supervisor, you can help your staff members manage the effects of vicarious trauma with a technique called "reframing"—a method of helping a person rethink a negative or self-defeating attitude or feeling. Reframing helps staff members cope with stressful events they can't change. Here are some examples of statements and reframing responses.

Read (or ask for volunteers to read) the *Examples of "reframing" responses* slide (S16). Facilitate a brief discussion using this question:

> What reactions might staff members have when a supervisor responds by "reframing"?

Conclude by saying:

> Most communities have emergency service workers trained to facilitate trauma-related interventions. Contact your local Emergency Preparedness Department, Mental Health Association, or Crisis Intervention Center to learn more about the resources available in your community.

Facilitate a brief discussion using this question:

> Has anyone experienced a very stressful or traumatic event in the workplace? If so, what was helpful in supporting staff members?

If a participant shares an experience, be aware that it might trigger some emotional response from them or other participants. Be mindful of the fact that other participants may also have experienced trauma, and they may still be recovering and unable to tolerate a prolonged discussion. Conclude the discussion with the idea that no one is invulnerable to this form of stress and encourage participants to take good care of themselves.

10.   Resolving conflict (30 min.)

Introduce this topic with an opening statement such as:

> There are times when being a leader feels like you're the rope used in a game of "tug of war." You are torn between the pressures to achieve outcomes for programs and the realities of funding limitations and staffing capacities. In attempting to juggle these competing demands, you can become enmeshed in a submission-aggression loop. Here's what a submission-aggression loop might look like in a supervisor-staff member relationship:

Review the *Submission-aggression loop in a supervisor-staff member relationship* slide (S17).

> In chapter 4, there is a comparison between the principles and practices of family development and the process of principled negotiation used in business. Let's review the comparison.

Review (or ask participants to review) the *Principles and practices of family development compared with principled negotiation* handout (H6).

> Conflict can have positive outcomes, if handled with skill and care. It can be a dynamic force, bringing problems to a head that have been festering beneath the surface. Conflict can keep things moving and force you to look at a situation from another person's point of view. It can even be an expression of caring. Apathy, not conflict, is the opposite of caring.

> We'll separate into two groups and each group will discuss a situation that involves resolving conflict. On one side of the room, a group will discuss a conflict between a supervisor and staff member; on the other side, the group will discuss a conflict among staff members in an interagency collaboration. Each group will write the four areas in principled negotiation: Guiding Principle, Communication, Facilitation, Conflict Resolution on easel paper. Then, referring to the Principles and Practices of Family Development, the group should use their knowledge of family development to generate ideas on how the leader or supervisor might resolve the conflict. Groups will have 10–15 minutes to discuss and prepare their ideas. Please designate a spokesperson to share your ideas when we reconvene.

In advance, make copies of the *Resolving conflict case studies* handout (H7). Read (or ask for volunteers to read) each case study. Designate one side of the room for each case study discussion group. Provide each group with easel paper and marker.

Circulate during the activity to provide encouragement or clarification. After about 10–15 minutes, ask the group to reconvene and ask the spokesperson to share the groups' ideas.

Facilitate a brief discussion using the following questions:

> 1. What strategies do you find most effective to address conflict?
>
> 2. Would anyone be willing to share an experience in which you successfully resolved a conflict using the principles and practices of family development?

H6

PRINCIPLED NEGOTIATION (FISHER AND URY, 1983[*])	PRINCIPLES AND PRACTICES OF FAMILY DEVELOPMENT (FOREST, 2015)
Guiding Principle: Separate the people from the problem.	*Guiding Principle*: Within every person, there is a bone-deep longing for freedom, self-respect, hope and the chance to make an important contribution to one's family, community and the world.
Communication: Focus on interests, not positions.	The Family Development model helps workers learn and practice these skills for communicating "with skill and heart": <ul><li>Empathy</li><li>Listening well</li><li>Mutual respect: assertiveness</li><li>Paraphrasing</li><li>"I" messages</li><li>Factual, emotional and solution-based feedback</li><li>Nonverbal body language</li></ul>
Facilitation: Invent options for mutual gain.	Family development workers learn and practice these techniques in group facilitation: <ul><li>Brainstorming</li><li>Rank ordering and priority setting</li><li>Constructive questioning</li><li>Summary statement</li><li>Helping groups make decisions</li></ul>
Conflict resolution: Insist on using objective criteria.	*In Empowerment Skills for Workers*, the Steps of Conflict Resolution teach workers and families skills to get to a "win-win" solution: <ul><li>Encourage the other person to describe their complaint fully.</li><li>Use effective communication skills</li><li>Affirm something that will help the situation.</li><li>Look for the need behind the problem</li><li>Together, come up with a list of solutions</li><li>Together, choose one that meets both needs.</li><li>Agree on a specific period of time to try out the solution.</li></ul>

[*] R. Fisher and W. Ury, *Getting to Yes: Negotiating Agreement Without Giving In* (New York: Penguin, 1983).

H7 Resolving Conflict case studies

Employee conflict

You are the supervisor of a family development program.

Six months ago, George, an employee you supervise, started working a second job to pay tuition for coursework to complete his community college degree. Over the past few months, you've noticed his work performance has markedly slipped. He has turned in late activity reports, called in sick frequently and asked to leave early on several occasions. Your overall sense is that his attention is not on his job when he is working. During a meeting to discuss the situation, he is initially defensive, then apologetic, and finally gave you assurances his performance would improve.

The agency's fiscal department has just informed you that George's program has failed to meet anticipated outcomes, and the agency won't be fully reimbursed for services to meet program expenses. You learn that the decrease in funding is due to a backlog in George's work over the past three months. If the program continues to perform under expectations, you'll need to lay off staff members. You need to plan what you'll say and do when you meet with George later today to discuss this situation.

Collaboration conflict

You are the executive director of an agency that uses a family development approach in supporting families.

A well-established collaboration your agency has with XYZ agency has been experiencing severe problems with conflicts between staff members in both agencies over the past six months. Your frontline supervisor and staff members believe that XYZ agency isn't doing their share of the work required to enroll and serve families. Compared with last year, the collaboration has served 25% fewer families, but it has achieved the projected outcomes for those families enrolled. The supervisor and staff members want you to consider terminating the collaboration or moving the collaboration to another agency. You have been aware of these difficulties in the past but thought they had been resolved. Based on this new information, it appears that XYZ has changed the way they are collaborating with your agency. You need to develop a plan to talk with staff members from XYZ to find out what is happening, and to determine how to help all staff members in the collaboration work more effectively to meet interagency goals.

11.   Handling blame, criticism, and difficulties with your supervisor (30 min.)

In advance of the session, copy and separate the sections of the *"I" message situation cards* (H8).

Introduce this topic and activity with a statement such as:

> When someone is blamed or criticized, it's natural to feel defensive and want to retaliate with additional blame and criticism. As a supervisor and leader, you may have to reprimand or confront a staff member with a situation they don't want to face or have an issue or disagreement with your own supervisor that needs to be addressed. How can you do this in a respectful way, while being sensitive to the power differential in the working relationship?

> Using "I" messages in difficult situations can help you to express your thoughts and feelings clearly and respectfully, and to avoid the destructive blame and criticism cycle that often occurs. Using "I" messages as a communication technique may feel (and sound) awkward at first; but with practice you'll be able to use them more naturally in ways that reflect your unique personality. Here's the basic format of an "I" message.

Read the *Basic format of an "I" message* slide (S18). Then review the *Responses to an "I" message* slide (S19). Copy enough "I" message cards for each person in the group to have one.

> Let's practice developing and delivering an "I" message. Each of these cards describes a situation in which an "I" message could be used. Each person will pick one card and formulate an "I" message. Then choose a partner and share your "I" message in response to each situation. After both of you have done that, talk about how you would continue if your "I" message elicited resistance or emotion. Try to work with someone you haven't worked with before. You'll have about 10 minutes for this activity.

After about 10 minutes, ask the group to reconvene. Ask for their reactions to using "I" messages and, if there's time, ask for a volunteer to share their "I" message. Facilitate a brief discussion using these questions:

1. How comfortable would you be using "I" messages with a staff member? How about using "I messages" with your supervisor?

2. If there is a difference, how can you increase your comfort in using "I" messages?

H8 "I" message situation cards

Your supervisor continually sends you work related e-mails after work hours and on weekends and it takes up time with family to read and sometimes respond to them.	A report was left on your desk at 4 p.m. with a note from your supervisor to complete by 9 a.m. the following morning. You have a personal commitment that evening that can't be rescheduled.
Most of the staff and frontline supervisors in your agency have been trained in the family development approach. However, the Executive Director, your supervisor, is still using a deficit orientation and has shown no interest in participating in a strength-based leadership training.	Each time you ask to meet with your supervisor to discuss an important issue, they are distracted by their phone and other staff members coming in to ask questions. As a result, nothing gets resolved and you leave thinking you will need to deal with the issue yourself.
More and more tasks and responsibilities at work are being assigned to you. You want to perform at a high level but feel like you are being spread too thin to do an adequate job.	You are committed to modeling the strength-based concepts that you learned in *Empowerment Skills for Leaders*. Your supervisor, who has not gone through the training is questioning some of your practices.
Morale and trust are low at your agency. The ED, your supervisor, is perceived as showing disrespect and disregard to certain staff members while favoring others which is creating a toxic work environment.	Your annual performance review was just completed by your supervisor. There were a few items that were critiqued which surprised you because they were never discussed with you prior to the review. There was also no opportunity for you to explain or provide information that may have resulted in a different overall rating.

Your supervisor wants to reduce staff in a program that is not meeting outcomes. You feel the program needs more time and support and that this decision may negatively affect your staff members' morale and productivity.	A staff member complains that you've singled them out and expect more than from other staff members in that program. You feel that you supervise all staff members based on their individual strengths and needs.
A co-worker disagrees with your opinion about employers conducting random drug testing and accuses you of being too liberal (or conservative).	A family member involved with your agency reports that a staff member was rude and disrespectful to them during a telephone conversation.
A colleague from an interagency collaboration implies that problems in achieving outcomes are due to under-performing by your staff members. You disagree with this but are equally concerned about the problem.	A colleague from an interagency committee remarks that they heard your agency has been difficult to work with in the past.
A colleague from an interagency committee asks you if your agency is having some problems because they heard that some senior staff members had recently left the agency.	An interagency colleague asks you to write them a personal reference for a graduate school application and you feel uncomfortable about doing it.

12.   Group dynamics in the workplace (30 min.)

Introduce this topic with a statement such as:

> Whether the group you lead consists of an entire agency, a department, a unit, or members of a work team, group dynamics will undoubtedly influence the group process. Interagency and systems collaboration brings leaders and workers from diverse agencies and backgrounds together. The complex tasks of collaboration, such as joint planning, resource pooling, and assessment of outcomes, requires that leaders know how to foster healthy group dynamics. Here is a perspective on group dynamics, based on a developmental model.

Read (or ask for volunteers to read) the *Developmental stages of a group* slide (S20).

> Looking at our experience in this group, let's discuss how each stage has progressed so far. Using the descriptions on the slide, how has our group developed its own group process?

Facilitate a discussion using these questions:

Forming: How did the group act at that stage?

Storming: What conflicts and challenges have arisen?

Norming: What are our group's unspoken rules or "norms?"

Performing: Have you seen evidence of this happening?

Adjourning: Have you thought about what will happen to the group at the end of the series? What feelings do you have?

Review (or ask volunteers to read) the *Suggestions to successfully manage dynamics of group development* slides (S21).

Conclude the discussion with the idea that a group develops and achieves its goals over time, through skillful facilitation, and creative discussion. The next section will present another way to help groups and organizations develop in creative and innovative ways.

13. Reflecting-in-Action, and Single- and Double-Loop Learning (30 min.)

Introduce this topic with a statement such as:

> Reflecting-in-action is the habit of reflecting during an interaction or situation to understand how your beliefs or values are affecting a goal.

> The study of organizational development describes two types of learning: single-loop and double-loop learning. Here's a diagram that illustrates the sequence that distinguishes the single- and double-loop learning processes.

Review the *Single- and double-loop learning in organizations* slide (S22), making the following points:

- *Single-loop learning* occurs when supervisors and leaders respond using a "stamping out brush fires" approach to goal setting. This approach creates a cycle of action and reaction that doesn't reflect seeing the "bigger picture" of organizational values and beliefs.

- *Double-loop learning* occurs when supervisors and leaders stop to think and reflect on the "bigger picture" when planning and setting goals. Their actions are based on clarifying their vision with the underlying values and mission of the organization.

Refer to the section in Chapter 4 on single- and double-loop learning (pp. 100–102), and review the diagrams as an example.

Ask participants to arrange themselves into two groups. Distribute the *Reflecting-in-action and single- and double-loop learning* worksheet (H9). In advance, copy and separate the *Reflecting-in-action and single- and double-loop learning case situations* worksheet and *Information for reflecting-In-action* slips (H10).

Assign one case situation from the reflecting-in-action case situations to each group. Ask each group to read the case study and fill in information to complete the single-loop learning diagram (Actions and Consequence boxes).

After five minutes or so, give each group a copy of the corresponding slip labeled "Information for reflecting-in-action" for that case situation. Ask them to write in their idea of the "Values and Beliefs" stated in the "Information for reflecting-in-action" and use it in depicting a double-loop learning diagram. Ask them to revisit the "Actions" and "Consequences" boxes to see if using these values and beliefs would change any actions or consequences that might result.

After about 10 minutes, ask each group to present the diagram and explain any differences between single- and double-loop actions and consequences.

Facilitate a brief discussion using these questions:

1. When values and beliefs of leaders and the agency are made explicit, how does this understanding impact actions and possible consequences?

2. How can supervisors and leaders help staff members develop skills to "reflect-in-action"?

H9 Worksheet: Reflecting-in-action and single- and double-loop learning

- *Single-loop learning*: Actions taken based on "cause and effect" thinking, which result in consequences that require new or continued action.

- *Double-loop learning*: Actions taken to develop and implement goals based on the underlying beliefs and values of the organization.

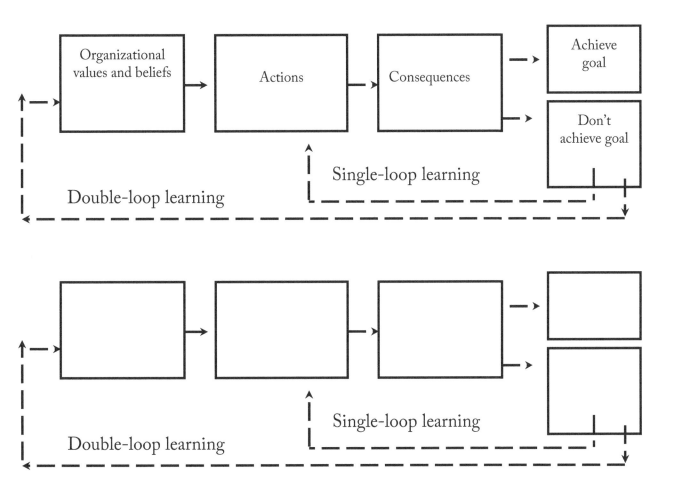

* The concepts of single- and double-loop organizational learning were developed by Chris Argyris and Donald Schon, *Organizational Learning II: Theory, Method and Practice* (Reading, MA: Addison-Wesley, 1996).

H10 Reflecting-in-action and single- and double-loop learning case situations

Directions: Copy and separate each section. Distribute one case situation to each group.

Case Situation 1

A long-established and valuable program in your agency has been chronically under-enrolled. The program doesn't serve enough families to sustain its required level of funding. Outreach to service partners and community stakeholders have provided some referrals, but not enough to keep the program going. Unless new steps are taken to increase enrollment, the funder will discontinue the program. Create a single-loop learning diagram to describe what has already occurred in this situation. Then, return to the "Action" box, and generate other ideas that could help resolve this problem.

Information for reflecting-in-action for Case Situation 1

You and other leaders in your agency believe that programs should be developed based on the ongoing assessment of families' and community needs. Your agency values the experiences and ideas of family members, staff members, and service partners when identifying ways to improve the agency's services.

Case Situation 2

There is an employment opening at your agency for a family development program supervisor. An experienced family worker in the program has applied, but they lack the supervisory experience and the formal education preferred for the position. Advertisements have not generated other qualified applicants. Past experience in hiring an applicant without supervisory experience and the desired educational credentials resulted in conflict among staff members and a sharp drop in achieving program outcomes. Create a single-loop learning diagram to describe what has already occurred in this situation. Then, return to the "Action" box, and generate other ideas that could help resolve this problem.

Information for reflecting-in-action for Case Situation 2

You and other leaders in your agency believe that all staff members have strengths, and that the type of support needed varies based on the situation and the skills of each person. The agency values family workers' strengths in setting goals for their own healthy self-reliance at work. The agency supports staff members in setting goals for their work performance and affirms that the role of the agency is to provide access to resources for staff members to reach their goals.

14.   Facilitating effective staff meetings and in-service training programs (30 min.)

Introduce this topic with a statement such as:

> Chapter 4 presents six advanced-level techniques to help supervisors and leaders facilitate discussion during a staff meeting or an in-service training program.

Read (or ask for volunteers to read) the *Techniques to facilitate creative small group discussion* slide (S23).

> We're going to practice one of these techniques, the Circle of Voices, responding to the question: What has been your greatest challenge in supervising with skill and heart?

Ask participants to arrange themselves into two groups (if the groups consist of more than eight members, separate them into three or more groups). Each group will designate a person as timekeeper. Ask groups to sit in a circle.

> Each person will have up to three minutes to talk. The discussion will go around the circle with the timekeeper keeping time. Each person can speak without interruption until the three minutes are up. After everyone has spoken, there is group discussion for about five minutes, but members can only talk about the ideas presented in the circle. Are there any questions?

Give a timeframe for the groups allowing three minutes per person and a five-minute open discussion time. Write the following question on easel paper: "What has been your greatest challenge in supervising with skill and heart?"

Circulate among the groups and observe how each group completes the activity. After the allotted time, ask the group to reconvene.

Facilitate a brief discussion using the following question:

> This technique is particularly helpful in getting all group members to share ideas. When could you use this technique with your staff members?

15. Planning for presenting Leadership Empowerment Plans (10 min.)

Discuss with the group that at the end of Chapter 5, there will be time allotted for each person to give a brief presentation to share what they plan to do for their Leadership Empowerment Plan including any initial progress that has occurred. Depending on the size of the group, decide on a time limit for each presentation in advance (e.g., 5–10 minutes), and answer any questions they may have.

Planning a cultural luncheon (optional)

Many groups have enjoyed a cultural luncheon as part of their session for Chapter 5, The Inclusive Workplace. If desired, invite participants to bring a food item or dish that is representative of their own cultural heritage. During the luncheon, ask each person to share with the group why they chose that food item or dish and how it represents their personal culture.

16. Planning Independent Learning Projects (30 min.)

Invite participants to spend a few minutes thinking about another project that will demonstrate and apply what they have learned in this chapter.

Ask them to find a partner with whom they will alternate the role of peer advisor and advisee. Ask them to get together and discuss their plans. Encourage them to support each other in setting a manageable plan and time frame to complete their projects.

17. Quick Feedback Form (10 min.)

In advance, make enough copies of the feedback form to distribute at the end of the session. Distribute the form and ask participants to complete and return it before they leave.

Empowerment Skills for Leaders

Chapter 4: Supervising with Skill and Heart

Quick Feedback Form

When during the session did you feel most engaged?

When during the session did you feel least engaged?

What would make your experience in this course better?

Thanks for your feedback!

Chapter 4 PowerPoint slides

Empowerment Skills for Leaders

Chapter 4: Supervising with Skill and Heart

Chapter 4: Learning Objectives

* Use "peripheral vision" to see strengths in staff members to better establish and build mutually respectful relationships.

* Expand your vision to see the "bigger picture" in goal setting and strategic planning.

* Determine how much personal information to share with staff members.

* Understand how to support staff during major organizational transitions.

* Increase awareness of and help staff manage workplace stress and job "burnout".

S1

Learning Objectives (continued)

* Seek support in helping staff cope with traumatic events.

* Practice conflict resolution skills using the principles and practices of family development.

* Understand the dynamics of group development in the workplace.

* Use creative discussion techniques in staff meetings and with other groups.

S1

About Perception

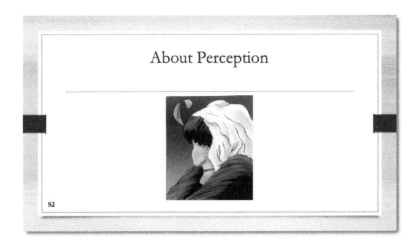

S2

Bifocal and Peripheral Vision

Bifocal Vision is the ability to see at two levels at the same time. For example, to see the reality of a situation along with the strengths, resources and opportunities.

Peripheral Vision is the ability to observe and find strengths, similarities and common ground with those you supervise. For example, taking a walk through your agency's office space as if you were a visitor.

S3

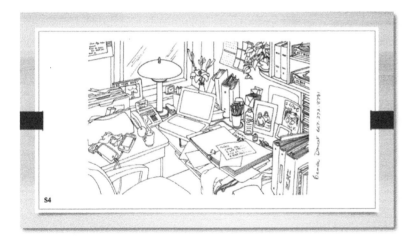

S4

Tunnel Vision

Tunnel Vision is the inability to see the peripheral or broader perspective.

Leaders with tunnel vision often spend too much time focusing on unimportant details or events that consume excessive amounts of energy.

"Reflecting in action" is reflecting *during* a situation to understand how your beliefs or values are affecting a goal. This approach can help you avoid "tunnel vision".

S5

Guidelines to help you decide what to share

➢ Be genuine.

➢ Offer empathy and share your own personal experience to build rapport.

➢ Don't rely on your colleagues to help solve your problems. Set up a good support system for yourself so that you don't become dependent on those with whom you work.

➢ Be prepared for anything you share to be discussed (and possibly distorted) by others.

➢ Share enough personal information so that co-workers can see that you're "real", but not so much that you become dependent on their discretion to keep important confidences.

S6

Guidelines for using strengths-based assessment with employees

❑ Collect the information you need to assess an employee's or team's efforts and accomplishments through a variety of sources.

❑ Help an employee (or team) identify a major goal along with the steps that you and they will take to achieve that goal.

❑ Assess performance based on criteria that you and the employee (or team) develop collaboratively in advance.

❑ Approach assessments with a strengths-based point of view. Look at performance issues as opportunities to learn and help develop skills.

S7

Strengths-based employee assessments

Incorporating five key areas in your performance review process

* Client satisfaction and loyalty to the organization's growth
* Teamwork and collaboration
* Open communication
* Interpersonal skills
* Adaptability to change

(David A. Russell, *Phrases for Performance Appraisals Resource Guide*)

S8

Situations in which employees may experience grief/loss

Terminations or lay-offs that leave remaining employees left with "survivor guilt".

Frequent employee turnover that requires remaining employees to constantly adjust to loss and change.

S9

Grief/loss situations (continued)

Reorganization that changes well established relationships with supervisors.

Promotions that change an employee's role from peer to supervisor of former co-workers.

Relocations or transfers that make it difficult for employees to maintain close relationships with former colleagues.

Workplace tragedy- loss of life or property (employee and/or family member).

Others?

S9

Typical grief responses

Physical Response- denial, disbelief, personalizing loss

Emotional Response- grief process and mourning

Psychological Response- memorializing the past relationship

Ongoing Adjustment- lifelong coping with cycles of grief

S10

Supporting employees during major transitions

* Be aware and responsive to the grief process that employees and teams experience as a result of a major transition or loss.

* Help employees express their feelings about the loss and provide practical assistance to make the transition smoother.

* Offer hope and encouragement whenever you can to help employees regain a sense of stability.

* Expect disruption and confusion in employee and team performance immediately before and after a major transition.

S11

Supporting employees during major transitions (continued)

* Understand that you may also be affected by a major transition or loss and take good care of yourself.

* Make referrals for employee assistance as appropriate

* Others?

S11

Potential contributors to job "burnout"

- Ongoing excessive workloads or consistently being required to perform at peak capacity without adjustments being made to other duties.
- Life-altering stresses in non-work areas that consume time and emotional energy.
- Working an excessive number of hours each week.
- Work duties that significantly underutilize a person's skills and abilities.
- Sedentary jobs or jobs that require more physical strength than a person can manage on a daily basis.

S12

Potential contributors to job burnout
(continued)

- Jobs with unclear expectations and unpredictable measures of accountability for results.
- Working in a physically or emotionally stressful workplace without having power to change the environment.
- Others?

S12

Symptoms of job "burnout"

Early stages of burnout:
- ✓ Low energy and feelings of extreme tiredness
- ✓ Frequent absenteeism
- ✓ Increased cynicism and decreased empathy

Later stages of burnout:
- ✓ Detachment from program participants and co-workers
- ✓ Withdrawal from activities previously enjoyed outside of work
- ✓ Lack of effort ultimately impacting job performance

S13

Situations that create risk for traumatic stress

❖ Personal and family catastrophes such as assault, rape, severe injury and loss of home due to fire, flood or natural disaster.

❖ A loved one or close friend being victimized by crime.

❖ Death of a co-worker, unexpectedly or in the line of work duty.

❖ Witnessing or responding to another person's catastrophe, being at the scene of an accident, assault, suicide or homicide.

❖ A mass shooting or other incidents of violence inside or outside the workplace.

S14

Symptoms of post-traumatic stress

Although post-traumatic stress can only be diagnosed and treated by trained, licensed professionals, symptoms can include:

Mental "flashbacks" or intrusive thoughts about an event or experience

Sleep disturbances (insomnia or lethargy)

Appetite changes (wanting to eat too much or too little)

Hypervigilance or oversensitivity to common occurrences (such as an extremely startled reaction to a loud noise)

S15

Examples of "reframing" responses

Reframing is a method of helping a person rethink a negative or self-defeating attitude or feeling. This method can address the following situations:

Overgeneralizing from one situation:

Statement: *"That agency didn't help me. The last time I called there, the worker didn't help me"*

Reframing Response: *"Perhaps the worker was having a bad day. I know the agency has been around a long time and I've heard they have a good reputation in the community."*

S16

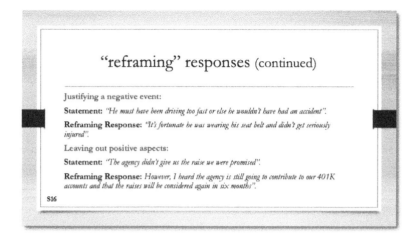

"reframing" responses (continued)

Justifying a negative event:

Statement: *"He must have been driving too fast or else he wouldn't have had an accident".*

Reframing Response: *"It's fortunate he was wearing his seat belt and didn't get seriously injured".*

Leaving out positive aspects:

Statement: *"The agency didn't give us the raise we were promised".*

Reframing Response: *However, I heard the agency is still going to contribute to our 401K accounts and that the raises will be considered again in six months".*

S16

Reframing Responses

R- Reframing

E- Encourages

F-Focus

R-Reduces

A- Anxiety

M-Models

E- Empathy

S16

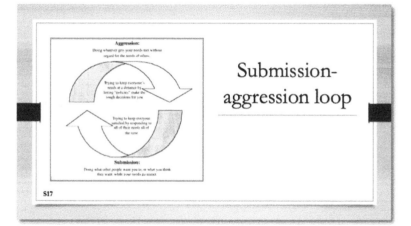

Submission-aggression loop

S17

Basic format of an "I" message

When_____ happens,

I feel_____

because _____.

I would like _____.

When you ask me to have that report to you first thing tomorrow and it's 4:30 now, it means I need to take work home. I feel frustrated because I had planned to spend time with my family this evening.

I would like to arrange my schedule to work on the report first thing tomorrow and have the report to you as soon as possible.

S18

Responses to an "I" message

Possible responses	Your response can be...
Compliance	Gracious acceptance (thank you for listening)
Resistance	Feedback, listening, restating your needs
Emotion	Emotional feedback, listening, restating your needs
An expression of their needs	Respect for their needs, use steps to resolve conflict, commitment to a "win-win" solution to the situation.

S19

Developmental Stages of a Group

1. Forming
* Time of orientation
* High degree of guidance needed from facilitator
* Process usually not well established

2. Storming
* Group members are determining roles and how decisions are made.
* Shared commitment and clear purpose is established
* Team relationships are still being worked out

S20

Developmental Stages of a Group (continued)

3. Norming

* Relationships are well understood by the team

* Commitment to team goals

* Team members begin working together to optimize team process

4. Performing

* Group efforts show progress in reaching outcomes

* Team members mediate differences to keep moving forward

* Little oversight is needed to maintain focus

S20

Suggestions to successfully manage dynamics of group development

Forming:

* Help members get to know one another formally and informally

* Set mutual expectations and clear boundaries for interaction

* Develop policies and procedures for regular feedback and ongoing assessment

* Increase group cohesion through activities that allow humor, nonjudgmental sharing and open discussion

Storming:

* Facilitate ways for team members to manage differing opinions and cultural differences in the group

* Provide opportunities to discuss and reflect on the costs and benefits of the program or collaboration for themselves and the organization.

S21

Suggestions to successfully manage dynamics of group development (continued)

Norming:

* Establish "shared power" norms for tasks and overall group outcomes

* Share relevant information with all group members to maintain transparency

Performing:

* Provide encouragement and reinforcement to the group

* Help members move beyond their "comfort zones" when necessary

* Acknowledge group and individual milestones and accomplishments

S21

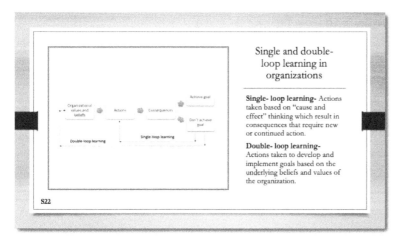

Single and double-loop learning in organizations

Single- loop learning- Actions taken based on "cause and effect" thinking which result in consequences that require new or continued action.

Double- loop learning- Actions taken to develop and implement goals based on the underlying beliefs and values of the organization.

S22

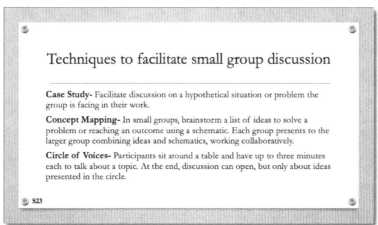

Techniques to facilitate small group discussion

Case Study- Facilitate discussion on a hypothetical situation or problem the group is facing in their work.

Concept Mapping- In small groups, brainstorm a list of ideas to solve a problem or reaching an outcome using a schematic. Each group presents to the larger group combining ideas and schematics, working collaboratively.

Circle of Voices- Participants sit around a table and have up to three minutes each to talk about a topic. At the end, discussion can open, but only about ideas presented in the circle.

S23

Techniques to facilitate small group discussion (continued)

Circular Response- Participants have three minutes to add their ideas to a structured discussion, but before adding their own ideas, they must first paraphrase comments offered by the previous person and build on those.

Snowballing- Pairs discuss a topic for a designated time. When time is up, the pairs combine with another pair for continued discussion and so on until the entire group is reconvened. The facilitator then processes with the group.

Rotating Small Group Stations- Small groups work together at posted stations around the room. After a designated time, each group moves to the next station, building on the ideas presented.

S23

CHAPTER 5
THE INCLUSIVE WORKPLACE

Teaching materials

- LCD projector/smart board, power points

- Easel, easel paper, and markers

- Masking, cellophane tape or self-sticking easel paper

- Copies of handouts/worksheets

- Melodic bell or chime (to reconvene the group)

- Cultural Luncheon supplies as needed (optional)

- Refreshments (optional)

	Activities	Approximate Duration (minutes)	Slides	Handouts/Materials
1	*Welcome, agenda, and Ch. 4 feedback summary*	10		
2	*Ch. 5 Learning Objectives*	5	S1 Learning objectives for Ch. 5	
3	*Warmup circle: "Who's here?"* *Familiar to me, familiar to you—Exploring the awareness of difference*	20 20		H1 Familiar to me, familiar to you
4	*Culture and multiculturalism*	30	S2 Definition of culture in a family development context S3 Multiculturalism Is…	H2 Multicultural matrix
5	*Cultural competence and cultural humility*	45	S4 Definition of cultural competence S5 Cultural humility S6 Excerpt from "On Caring" by Milton Mayeroff	H3 Cultural assessment case studies
6	*Understanding your unique cultural identity*	45	S7 Historical influences in our lifetime S8 "Melting pot" or "salad bowl"	H4 Your personal "grand mosaic"
7	*Your agency's organizational culture*	45	S9 Public aspects of organizational culture S10 Private aspects of organizational culture	H5 Worksheet: Assessing your agency's organizational culture
8	*Organizational cultural competence and inclusiveness*	30	S11 Definition of organizational cultural competence and inclusiveness S12 Guidelines for developing your organization's cultural competence	
9	*Barriers to organizational cultural competence and cultural humility*	45	S13 Barriers to organizational cultural competence and cultural humility	H6 Barriers to organizational cultural competence case situations H7 Reflecting on the barriers to organizational cultural competence and humility

Activities	Approximate Duration (minutes)	Slides	Handouts/Materials
10 *Clashes between organizational and family cultures*	20		H8 Clashes between organizational and family cultures situations H9 Worksheet: Reflecting on clashes between organizational and family cultures
11 *Developing an inclusive organization*	30	S14 Ways to develop your organization's multicultural competence S15 Questions on ways to develop organizational multicultural competence	
12 *Interagency collaboration*	30		H10 Carmen and Yvette's second meeting
13 *Family Development Leadership Model*	20–30	S16 Family Development Leadership Model	H11 Family Development Leadership Model
14 *Sharing the Leadership Empowerment Plans*	TBD		
15 *Planning Independent Learning Projects*	30		
16 *Final Feedback Form*	10		Final Feedback Form

Supplemental Resources

There are resources at the end of each chapter in the *Empowerment Skills for Leaders* Handbook. A suggestion would be to select one of the articles listed (or another of your choice) that you feel is relevant and of interest to the group and distribute copies for them to read (or refer them to a link online) before the next class session. At the beginning of the next class session, facilitate a brief discussion about the article and how it reinforces the concepts covered in the chapter.

Links to additional resources are on the FDC website, www.familydevelopmentcredential.org, under Instructor Resources.

Videos

Jones, Dewitt. "Celebrate What's Right with the World." TEDxSouthLakeTahoe. YouTube video, 18:10. Posted 3 January 2018. https://www.youtube.com/watch?v=gD_1Eh6rqf8.

PBS. *Latino-Americans*. Video series. Washington, DC: WETA, 2013. https://www.pbs.org/latinoamericans/en/watch-videos/ - 2365075996.

PBS. *Race: The Power of an Illusion*. Three-part documentary about race in society, science and history. Produced by California Newsreel. https://www.pbs.org/race/000_General/000_00-Home.htm.

Audio

NPR. "The Culture Inside." *Invisibilia*. Podcast series, 2017. https://www.npr.org/programs/invisibilia/532950995/the-culture-inside.

Websites

California Newsreel is a source for several excellent videos: http://www.newsreel.org.

Gassam, Janice. Videos on diversity, inclusion, and workplace trends related to diversity and inclusion. https://www.drjanicegassam.com.

Southern Poverty Law Center has some excellent free resources and films with teaching guides. They also have a project called "Teaching Tolerance": https://www.splcenter.org/teaching-tolerance.

Washington, Ella, and Camille Patrick. *3 Requirements for a Diverse and Inclusive Culture*. Gallup, September 17, 2018. https://www.gallup.com/workplace/242138/requirements-diverse-inclusive-culture.aspx.

Optional cultural luncheon

You may want to incorporate a cultural luncheon for participants during which they can share food that represents their heritage or cultural background. In advance of this session, ask participants if they would like to do this. If they agree, ask for volunteers to provide beverages or paper products as needed.

During the luncheon, facilitate relaxed and informal sharing of experiences related to food, customs, and cultural traditions. Other ideas for cultural sharing may include wearing or bringing an item to the session that represents an aspect of a participant's culture; asking volunteers to talk about a cultural tradition such as Kwanzaa, Hanukkah, or Ramadan; or arranging for a guest speaker on a topic of interest to the group.

Activities

1.   Welcome, agenda, and feedback summary (10 min.)

Begin the session by welcoming everyone back.

Provide a short summary of feedback from the last session, highlighting positive comments. Discuss any feedback that you think the group needs to process or give you further information on.

2.   Chapter 5 Learning Objectives (5 min.)

Read (or ask for volunteers to read) the *Chapter 5 Learning Objectives* slides (S1).

- Practice the skills necessary to develop increased cultural humility and inclusiveness in the workplace.

- Understand the benefits and challenges of multiculturalism in a changing American society.

- Explore elements of your personal cultural identity.

- Take steps to strengthen cultural sensitivity and inclusiveness in the workplace.

- Identify aspects of your agency's organizational culture.

- Recognize barriers to achieving multicultural competence and inclusiveness in the workplace.

- Understand how differences in organizational culture may impact collaborative efforts.

- Develop and implement a Leadership Empowerment Plan that encompasses the strength-based principles of family development.

3.   Warmup Activity: "Who's Here?" Circle (20–40 min.)

Introduce the warm-up activity with a statement such as:

> Each person has a unique cultural history. Some elements stay the same throughout our life like race or first language and others can change like family form and religion. We're all influenced by our families, traditions, life experiences, and cultural groups. This is a quick and fun activity to learn more about our personal cultural identities as a group.

Designate an open area or create space to stand in a circle. Then continue:

> This activity is called the "Who's Here? Circle." To begin, let's stand in a circle. I'll call out an aspect of a cultural identity and if that cultural identity applies to you, you are welcome to step into the circle. After everyone steps in who wants to, I'll invite you to step back out to hear the next category. If you want, you can call out additional categories at the end, but they must apply to you.

One by one, call out this list of cultural identities. Feel free to add or delete from this list as appropriate. Begin with the statement:

> You are invited to step into the circle if you:
> - are of African American heritage
> - are of African heritage
> - are of Native American heritage
> - are of Hispanic heritage
> - are of Latino heritage
> - are of European heritage
> - are of another ethnic heritage (invite the person to identify the ethnic heritage)
> - are of more than one ethnic heritage
> - speak English as your home language
> - speak another language as your home language
> - speak more than one language
> - speak more than two languages
> - have lived in the state where you now reside since birth or childhood
> - moved to the state where you live now from another part of the United States
> - moved to the United States from another country
> - grew up in a military family
> - live with a partner or spouse
> - live with children
> - live alone
> - live with pets
> - live with other family members or someone whom you consider family

Invite the group to call out other categories that apply to them and invite others to step in the circle. When finished, thank the group for their participation.

Familiar to Me, Familiar to You—Exploring the awareness of difference (20 min.)

As an alternative or addition to the "Who's Here?" Circle warmup, FDC Instructor Angela Zimmerman, from Molloy College, Long Island, created the "Familiar to Me, Familiar to You" exercise for her classes.[*]

Introduce the activity with a statement such as:

> **We are all unique individuals. However, getting to know and learning more about others helps us to see the commonalities as well as the differences.**

Distribute the *Familiar to Me, Familiar to You* worksheet (H1). Ask the group to identify 5-10 things that are familiar to them and common to their everyday life. Examples could be foods they eat, music, daily routines, etc. List these in the Familiar to Me column. Then find a partner to share their lists, writing their partner's items in the Familiar to You column. Discuss the similarities and differences.

Allowing enough time for sharing, process the activity with the group.

[*] Thanks to Angela Zimmerman for suggesting this activity.

H1 Worksheet: Familiar to Me, Familiar to You

Identify 5 to 10 things that are familiar to you and common to your everyday life. Think of things like the foods you eat, music you listen to, TV shows you watch, places you visit for fun, etc. List these items in the Familiar to Me column. Then, find a partner and ask them to share some things from their list with you and write them down in the Familiar to You column. Discuss with your partner the similarities and differences.

Familiar to Me	Familiar to You

4.   Culture and multiculturalism (30 min.)

Introduce this topic and activity with a statement such as:

> When we think of a person's culture, it's common to think of the traditional definition of culture as an attribute or observable trait such as race, religion, or economic status. And while those qualities are part of a person's culture, today's definition of culture also encompasses less visible aspects such as the attitudes, beliefs, values, and customs held or practiced by a particular social, racial, religious, or ethnic group. Here is the definition of "culture" used in family development training.

Read (or ask for a volunteer to read) the *Definition of culture in a family development context* slide (S2):

> The term multiculturalism has been used to describe the reality that society is comprised of a diversity of cultures.

Review the *Multiculturalism Is* slide (S3). Make the points below:

> Today we live in a multicultural society. In the chapter, Nathan Glazer proposes that we are all multiculturalists: People influenced by, while at the same time, influencing, and shaping their culture. For example, your personal experiences influence your beliefs and values which, in turn, affect how you interact with others. Multiculturalism can be depicted as a matrix in which intersecting variables come together. Here is what a matrix of intersecting cultural variables might look like.

Distribute the *Multicultural Matrix* handout/worksheet (H2). Then continue:

> Each box in the matrix highlights a point at which two aspects of a person's culture meet. For example, the first box is the intersection of a person's gender with their beliefs. The question in that box states: "Does gender affect what is important in my life? If so, how?"

> To explore how these aspects and variables affect our lives, pick a row or column on the Multicultural Matrix and fill it out. When finished, find a partner and share your responses with each other for about ten minutes. Choose more than one column or row to complete and share, if you like.

After about 10 minutes, ask the group to reconvene. Facilitate a brief discussion using these questions:

1. Why is it helpful for supervisors and leaders to understand how different variables (e.g. gender or race) affect cultural identity and attitudes?

2. How is your agency adapting its services to offer family support in a multicultural society?

H2 Worksheet: Multicultural Matrix

	GENDER	RACE	SOCIAL CLASS	ETHNICITY
Your Beliefs	How does gender affect what's important in your life?	How does race affect what's important in your life?	How does social class affect what's important in your life?	How does ethnicity affect what's important in your life?
Your Values	How does your gender influence what you value in life?	How does your race influence what you value in life?	How does your social class influence what you value in life?	How does your ethnicity influence what you value in life?
Your Customs	How does your gender affect the way you live?	How does your race affect the way you live?	How does your social class affect the way you live?	How does your ethnicity affect the way you live?
Your Actions	How does your gender affect the way you act?	How does your race affect the way you act?	How does your social class affect the way you act?	How does your ethnicity affect the way you act?

5.   Cultural competence and cultural humility (45 min.)

On a piece of easel paper, write the sentence fragment: "A culturally competent person…" Ask the group to share ideas that complete the statement. Write down their responses.

Then continue:

> Cultural competence is more than simply recognizing what makes people unique and different from one another. Here is a definition of cultural competence.

Read (or ask a volunteer to read) the *Definition of cultural competence* slide (S4).

> Cultural humility goes beyond cultural competence delving deeper into self-reflection. Cultural humility is having a humble and respectful attitude toward individuals of other cultures that pushes us to challenge our own personal biases and realize that we can't possibly know everything about other cultures. It's a lifelong process.

Review the *Cultural humility* slide (S5).

> This segment of the poem "On Caring" by Milton Mayeroff describes some ways to practice cultural competence and cultural humility.

Read (or ask for a volunteer to read) the *"On Caring" by Milton Mayeroff* slide (S6). Then facilitate a brief discussion using this question:

> Do you think this is true? Can you possibly "understand them and their world as if you were inside it?"

Continue with:

> Developing cultural competence and cultural humility is a lifelong process; it involves learning and honoring the culture of others while exploring and honoring your own. We learn about other cultures in a variety of ways. This activity will help you explore another person's cultural experience. Let's divide into four groups. I'll give each group a statement/case study made by a person that reflects their cultural experience.
>
> Ask yourself: "Who is the person writing this?" What is this person's gender, age, ethnicity, etc.? What else do you think you know?
>
> After 10 minutes, we'll reconvene. Designate a group spokesperson to read the description and share your group's ideas with the larger group.

Arrange participants into four groups, and distribute one of the *Cultural assessment case studies* (H3) to each group. Circulate during the activity to answer questions or clarify information. If groups are troubled by the lack of in-depth information, remind them that cultural humility doesn't require that we know everything about a person in advance, but that we respond based on our current understanding.

After about 10 minutes, ask the group to reconvene. Ask each group's spokesperson to read the case study, then share the cultural description of the individual they developed. Facilitate a brief discussion using this question:

> **How can you learn about and honor other cultures? What questions would you ask?**

H3 Cultural assessment case studies

When I grow up, I wanna be a teacher. Teachers are nice. They get to write on the blackboard. They make things with colored paper and crayons and glue. Teachers give you a star or a stamp on your paper when you do good. My teacher has a pretty smile. She helps me when I don't know things. My teacher says everybody should try and do their best. Sometimes when we're really good, she gives us a piece of candy.

I like hangin' out with my friends or just watching TV. Sometimes we play some ball or just sit around talkin'. We don't really talk about anything big—we're just hangin' out. Parents don't really understand. My friends are there for me. We spend hours talking about the game last night, what clothes you wouldn't be caught dead wearing or things at school. If we fight over something, you chill out for a few days. Then you just see each other and you're friends again, like nothing happened.

Being a family worker is really rewarding, but at the same time, it can be stressful. Helping families see their strengths and make progress on their goals is the best part. Life can deal some pretty bad cards to some families. Take one of the families I've been working with. They were just getting back on their feet after a rough time when the mother found out she has a serious illness. That's the hard part of the job.

I didn't really set out to be a family worker. I tell people it found me. I really care about the families I work with. I've had some tough times myself through the years so I can relate. I think families need to know someone cares about them. And to help keep their hope alive that things will get better.

The hardest part about being alone after my wife died is having no one to talk to. This is a big place for just one person now. I'm pretty self-sufficient—I do my own cooking, laundry. Until she passed, I never done those things before in my life. I even help at the center taking meals to shut-ins a few times a week. Everybody's got some troubles. I'm not angry. We had a good life together. Sometimes I just wish I had someone to go places with and talk to.

6.   Understanding your unique cultural identity (45 min.)

Introduce this topic with a statement such as:

> Cultural identity refers to an individual's experience of their culture within a historical, social or environmental context. Your cultural identity is unique and distinct from any other person, even someone who may have similar cultural characteristics.

> The impact of historical events can influence personal cultural identity. Here's a list of some of the social movements and events that have shaped American culture over the past century:

Read (or ask for a volunteer to read) the *Historical influences in our lifetime* slide (S7). Facilitate a discussion using these questions:

> 1.   Choose one of these influences. How has this influence affected your cultural identity? How did it affect your parents' cultural identity?
>
> 2.   What historical influences (those on the list or not) will affect the cultural identity of future generations?

Continue:

> Another part of cultural identity is nationality or ethnic heritage. American culture has evolved through the process of blending a wide diversity of cultural groups. Part of your cultural identity has, no doubt, been influenced by your ancestors' experiences as they became acculturated and/or assimilated into the existing American culture.

Read (or ask for volunteers to read) the *"Melting pot" or "salad bowl"* slide (S8). Facilitate a brief discussion using this question:

> What are the costs and benefits of both acculturation and assimilation?

Continue:

> The journey to cultural competence begins with you. By exploring your own cultural identity, you gain a deeper understanding of yourself and others.

> Your cultural identity is made up of many parts such as ethnicity, heritage, and the influence of historical events. But it is also more than the sum of those parts. Just as the American culture could be described as a "grand mosaic," your personal cultural identity is also a "grand mosaic" of all the influences that make you a unique individual. This activity will look at the components of your personal "grand mosaic."

Distribute the *Your personal "grand mosaic"* worksheet (H4). Then continue:

> I'll lead the group slowly through each piece of the mosaic so that everyone has time to write. You're welcome to write in whatever response you feel fits that category.

Read through each statement allowing enough time in between each one for the group to reflect and write their response:

Write down the following items:

- An aspect of your cultural identity that other people can see
- An aspect of your cultural identity that others can't see about you
- An aspect of your cultural identity that you are proud of
- An aspect of your cultural identity that is difficult for you
- An aspect of your culture that comes from your ancestors
- An aspect of your cultural identity that you developed in childhood
- An aspect of your cultural identity that you developed completely on your own
- An aspect of your cultural identity that you want to preserve as your legacy for the future

Invite them to share their grand mosaic with the person next to them for a few minutes, with the reminder to honor and respect their own comfort level in sharing their responses.

Conclude by asking for general reactions to completing this activity and with a brief discussion on the following question:

If you removed a piece of your mosaic, how would it change your cultural identity? How might you think or act differently without this piece?

H4 Worksheet: Your personal "Grand Mosaic"

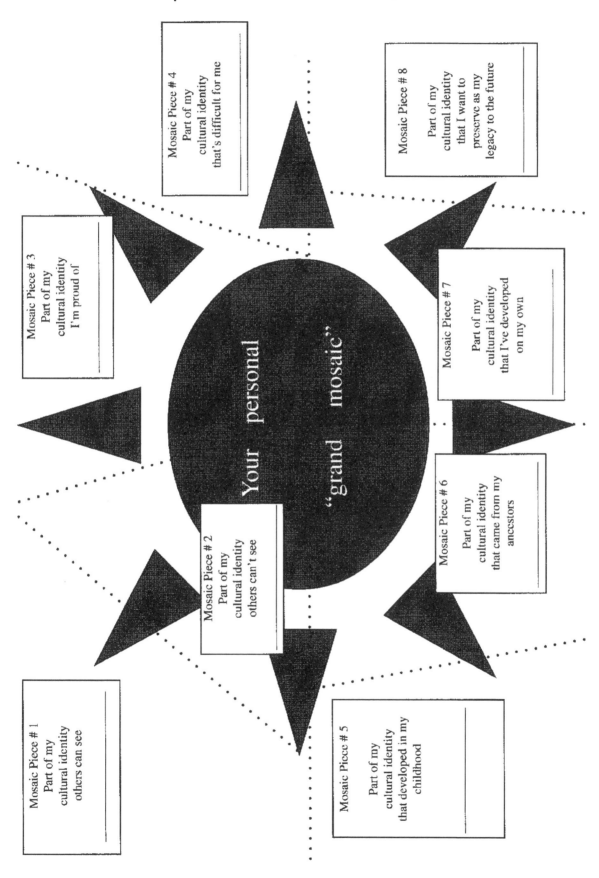

Mosaic Piece # 4
Part of my
cultural identity
that's difficult for me

Mosaic Piece # 8
Part of my
cultural identity
that I want to
preserve as my
legacy to the future

Mosaic Piece # 3
Part of my
cultural identity
I'm proud of

Mosaic Piece # 7
Part of my
cultural identity
that I've developed
on my own

Your   personal
"grand   mosaic"

Mosaic Piece # 2
Part of my
cultural identity
others can't see

Mosaic Piece # 6
Part of my
cultural identity
that came from my
ancestors

Mosaic Piece # 1
Part of my
cultural identity
others can see

Mosaic Piece # 5
Part of my
cultural identity
that developed in my
childhood

7.   Your agency's organizational culture (45 min.)

Introduce this topic with a statement such:

> An organization's culture, like a person's culture, is comprised of many components. And just as an individual develops a personal cultural identity, most organizations develop a unique identity that translates into an organizational culture. Here are some public aspects of culture found in most organizations:

Read (or ask volunteers to read) the *Public aspects of organizational culture* slide (S9). Facilitate a brief discussion using this question, and record the responses on easel paper:

> What slogans, symbols, or practices does your organization use to communicate its organizational culture?

Continue:

> The aspects we've just discussed communicate public information to families, supporters, collaborators, funders, and the community. There are also aspects of organizational culture that communicate internal or private information to staff members, supervisors, and leaders. Here are some private aspects of culture in most organizations:

Read (or ask for volunteers to read) the *Private aspects of organizational culture* slide (S10). Distribute copies of the *Assessing your agency's organizational culture* worksheet (H5).

> This worksheet helps you assess some internal aspects of your agency's organizational culture. Read each statement and place an "X" on the continuum to indicate where your agency is currently positioned.

> Then, based on where you place the "X" on the continuum for each statement, complete the four sentences at the bottom of the page with statements reflecting the direction and strength of each response.

> If you place an "X" on the center line, it means that you believe your agency is equally focused between the two dimensions. In the sentences at the bottom of the page, you can also use a descriptor to state where "X" is located along the continuum. For example, if you place an "X" on Statement 1 near the left end of the continuum, you could finish the statement in one of two ways:

> - "My organization is currently focused on staff members acting with a great deal of individual responsibility."

> Or...

> - "My organization is currently focused on staff members acting with very little or no team accountability."

> Take five minutes to do the worksheet and then we'll continue our discussion.

While participants complete the worksheet, post four sheets of easel paper with continuum headings from each statement. For example, label the first sheet "Individual Responsibility" and "Team-oriented Accountability" (see the sample below). Under each heading, make columns labeled "Advantages" and "Disadvantages." Label the other sheets using the headings from Statements 2, 3 and 4 with columns for advantages and disadvantages.

Individual Responsibility		Team-Oriented Accountability	
Advantages	Disadvantages	Advantages	Disadvantages

It's important to remember that every organization has its own culture. A value, habit, or practice used by one organization may not work for another even if the organizations are similar. For this reason, identifying the advantages and disadvantages can help us understand and respect another organization's culture.

Around the room, I've posted the four continuums you just completed on the worksheet. For the next ten minutes, circulate to each sheet and referring to your worksheet, write either an advantage or disadvantage of that aspect based on your experience in your organization.

After about 10 minutes, ask the group to reconvene. Ask for volunteers to read and review each of the sheets. Facilitate a brief discussion using these questions:

This activity helps clarify your perception of some private aspects of your organization's culture.

1. What information could you learn if staff members, other leaders, or key advisors completed this assessment?

2. If there is an aspect of your organizational culture that you would like to change, how would you begin changing it?

H5 Worksheet: Assessing your agency's organizational culture

Directions: Read the four statements below and place an "X" on the continuum to indicate where you think the culture of your agency is positioned right now. Then, complete the sentences on the next page with a description that reflects the direction and strength of each response.

Statement 1

My organization is currently focused on staff members acting with…

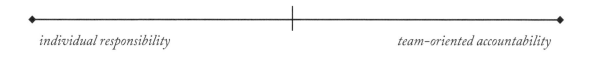

individual responsibility   *team-oriented accountability*

Statement 2

The majority of staff members in my organization feel the agency…

promotes personal and career development   *deters personal and career development*

Statement 3

Most of my organization's services and programs are currently offered to the community.

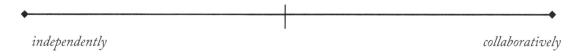

independently   *collaboratively*

Statement 4

Most staff members believe our agency to be…

paternalistic/maternalistic   *entrepreneurial*

Current assessment of my agency's organizational culture

1. My organization currently focuses on staff members acting with…

    _____

2. The majority of staff members in my organization feel that the agency…

    _____

3. Most of my organization's services and programs are currently offered to the community.

    _____

4. Most staff members believe our agency to be…

    _____

8.   Organizational cultural competence and inclusiveness (30 min.)

Introduce this topic and activity with a statement such as:

> Here is an adaptation of the earlier cultural competence definition presented in an organizational context.

Read (or ask for volunteers to read) the *Definition of organizational cultural competence and inclusiveness* slide (S11):

> This definition describes organizational cultural competence as the collective ability of leaders (supervisors) and staff members to learn from and relate respectfully to other organizational cultures.

Facilitate a brief discussion using this question:

> Why do leaders, supervisors and staff members all need to work together to develop their organization's cultural competence?

Then continue:

> Here are some general guidelines for leaders, supervisors, and staff members to develop their organization's cultural competence together.

Read (or ask for a volunteer to read) the *Guidelines for developing your organization's cultural competence and inclusiveness* slide (S12).

Have participants arrange themselves into two groups. Indicate an imaginary center line down the center of the room to create two groups or use another method). Have each group generate ideas and record them on easel paper.

- Instruct one group to brainstorm specific ways or action steps that leaders and supervisors could use to develop their organization's cultural competence.

- Have the other group brainstorm specific ways or action steps that staff members could use to develop their organization's cultural competence.

Tell participants:

> Generate specific ideas you might actually use in your organization. Take 5 to 10 minutes and designate a spokesperson to present the ideas to the larger group.

After about 5 to 10 minutes, ask the group to reconvene. Ask each group's spokesperson to present their ideas. Facilitate a brief discussion using these questions:

1. How did the ideas for leaders/supervisors differ from those for staff members?

2. What strengths does each group bring to the goal of developing an organization's cultural competence?

9.   Barriers to organizational cultural competence and cultural humility (45 min.)

Introduce this topic and activity with a statement such as:

> One reality of living in a multicultural society is that there are barriers to achieving cultural competence and cultural humility, such as privilege, prejudice, discrimination, and oppression. The missions of most family support organizations include the goal of counteracting the hardships and negative impacts that these barriers impose on families. Barriers that exist in the larger culture can also be found in the workplace. Here are the four barriers to cultural competence and cultural humility adapted to an organizational context:

Read (or ask a volunteer to read) the *Barriers to organizational cultural competence and cultural humility* slide (S13).

> To explore specific ways these barriers can affect supervisors, leaders, and staff members, we will discuss four case situations. Each situation involves a supervisor or leader who confronts a cultural barrier in their workplace.
>
> After we read the situations, I'll designate areas for small group discussion and provide a list of questions. I'll ask you to choose a situation and go to that area to discuss it. Each group will generate ideas to share with the larger group. Take 10 minutes to develop your ideas. Please designate a spokesperson to share ideas with the larger group when we reconvene.

Distribute copies of the *Barriers to organizational cultural competence and cultural humility case situations* handout (H6). Assign each group a case situation and designate an area of the room for each group to meet. Distribute the *Reflecting on the barriers to organizational cultural competence and cultural humility* worksheet (H7) to each sub-group. Circulate during the small group discussion.

After about 10 minutes, ask the group to reconvene. Ask each spokesperson to read their case situation and share the ideas discussed. Facilitate a brief discussion using these questions:

---

1. What other barriers to cultural competence and cultural humility in organizations have you experienced?

2. What suggestions or recommendations would you offer to another supervisor or leader if barriers such as these are present?

H6 Case situations: Barriers to workplace cultural competence and cultural humility

Case situation 1

Myrna is the principal of an urban middle school. In recent months, she's felt that the usual climate of collegial friendship between her and teachers has been getting colder, more guarded, and distant. The "open door" policy she instituted three years ago when she became principal has turned into a daily series of "gripe sessions" for teachers and staff members.

New mandates and directives have recently required her to attend frequent meetings away from school. The district has applied for a large technology grant that also required her input and attention when she is in the office. She's noticed that when teachers and staff members stop at her office to leave a message, they are surprised to find her there. She realizes that morale has dropped and that she must do something to help teachers regain their sense of support and confidence in her leadership.

Case situation 2

Paolo was recently promoted to unit supervisor of the large human service agency in which he's worked for the past eight years. In this position, he now supervises former co-workers, some of whom have worked with the agency for more than twenty years.

The agency has affirmative action policies and he's aware that other workers in his department also applied for the position. When presenting new ideas to innovate some outdated procedures at his first staff meeting as supervisor, he noticed that his former colleagues appeared resistant to making changes and that they were writing notes to each other while he was speaking. He realizes that he needs to address the tensions in his relationships with former co-workers to be able to supervise effectively.

Case situation 3

Tim is a programmer and software developer for a large, successful computer technology company. His partner, David, is a graphic artist who was laid off from his job recently and has decided to start his own business. Tim's company offers good employee benefits, but it has been resistant to adding provisions in coverage for same-sex partners.

Tim has met with the human resource director to discuss this and shared information about other technology companies that provide similar coverage. The human resource director told him that including same-sex partners in the employee's benefits package is too expensive. Tim feels that he should be able to enroll in the same type of health insurance plan that employees with spouses and children have. He enjoys his job but thinks if he takes his request to company executives, there will repercussions in relationships with his supervisor and co-workers.

Case situation 4

Hannah is a sales representative for a fast-growing pharmaceutical company. Over the past two years, she's been one of the company's top performers and brought in several new corporate clients. Taking advantage of intensive training and incentive programs, she was able to market new product lines to well-established clients.

When her supervisor transferred to become regional sales manager in another state, she felt she had all the qualifications and experience to take his place. When she interviewed for the position, she got the impression the company was hesitant to send a woman to sales conferences and on extended out-of-town business trips. Instead, Joel, a sales rep with less experience and average sales quotas, got the position.

Hannah feels her initiative and work performance compared with other applicants was more than sufficient for advancement in the company. She was hoping to pursue a long-term career with this company, but she feels this experience is an indicator that advancement isn't based on developing her work-related skills and improving her capabilities.

H7 Worksheet: Reflecting on barriers to organizational cultural competence and cultural humility

1. Which barrier is illustrated in this case situation?

2. What are the beliefs, attitudes, and values exhibited by the main character? What impact do these factors have on this barrier?

3. What are some of the beliefs, attitudes, and values of the other characters? What impact do these factors have on this barrier?

4. What steps could the main character take to address/resolve the situation?

10. Clashes between organizational and family cultures (20 min.)

Introduce this topic with a statement such as:

> A major benefit for organizations that encourage cultural competence and cultural humility is that staff members become more aware of the impact of their own cultural identity on families. However, workers are often in a "no win" position if their agency's policies and procedures conflict with the values and customs of a family's culture.

Facilitate a brief discussion using this question:

> Can you describe an instance in which a family's culture clashed with your organization's culture?

Distribute the *Clashes between organizational and family cultures situations* handout (H8).

> Here are two situations that highlight clashes between organizational and family cultures. After we read them, find a partner, choose one situation, and spend ten minutes discussing the questions on the *Reflecting on clashes between organizational and family cultures* worksheet (H9).

Read (or ask for a volunteer to read) the two situations on the handout. Ask participants to choose a partner and discuss the questions.

After about 10 minutes, ask the group to reconvene. Recap the first situation and ask for volunteers to share their responses to the questions. Do the same for the second situation.

Facilitate a brief discussion using this question:

> What suggestions or recommendations would you give to a new supervisor if they needed to support a staff member experiencing a clash between the family's and the organization's cultures?

H8 Clashes between organizational and family cultures situations

Situation 1

You are a department director in a large family-serving organization. A frontline supervisor asks to meet with you to discuss difficulties family workers are having with several new immigrant families. These families have recently arrived as refugees. Their culture prohibits women from working outside the home or advancing their education.

Workers are frustrated because home visits can only be scheduled when men are at home, and women and children are not allowed to share in family decisions. In some cases, workers have been unable to provide services because they couldn't get information, or because the family was unwilling to change their customs in order to qualify for services.

Situation 2

You are the principal of a rural middle school. A teacher asks to meet with you to discuss a problem arranging a parent-teacher conference with an immigrant family. The student's parents have limited English speaking skills, and they operate a family business in which the student spends most of his time after school and on weekends.

The student has failing grades; his homework assignments look hastily prepared and incomplete. He appears well dressed and cared for and has had only occasional absences. He says he enjoys being with his parents at work. He has a younger sibling in the elementary school.

It's clear to you that unless he receives more support with his studies, he will fail and have to repeat the grade next year. The teacher says that he has developed strong friendships with peers in his class this year. The teacher feels that the family's work ethic interferes with his ability to focus on his studies.

H9 Worksheet: Reflecting on clashes between organizational and family cultures

1. What are some issues related to this clash between the organization's and family's culture?

2. What are this family's strengths?

3. How would you advise your staff member?

4. What could you do to resolve this situation?

11.   Developing an inclusive organization (30 min.)

Introduce this topic and activity with a statement such as:

> The methods to develop cultural competence and cultural humility on a personal level have much in common with the steps an organization can take to develop its multicultural competence. For staff members in organizations, multicultural competence involves exploring and honoring their organization's culture while learning about other organizations' cultures.

> Organizations develop an inclusive workplace over time and staff members' skills, once mastered, must be continually updated. Supervisors, leaders and staff members can expect to experience feelings of frustration and confusion during the process. But the benefits of working toward multicultural competence in your organization can be enormous. Here are some ways in which you can help develop your agency's multicultural competence:

Read (or ask for a volunteer to read) the *Ways to develop organizational multicultural competence* slide (S14).

> To explore some of the experiences you may have had in developing your agency's multicultural competence, we'll use the "snowballing" technique, using a set of questions that I'll give you.

Note

"Snowballing" is facilitated at a lively pace so that participants can share an idea without time for others to critique it. Similar to brainstorming, this group sharing technique is based on spontaneity. Adjust the three-minute time limit to keep participants alert and engaged.

As the group gets larger, "side conversations" naturally form. Encourage participants who aren't talking with anyone to "listen in" on side conversations and try to join in. This technique is intended to help participants focus on real-life experiences by changing the orientation of discussion from facilitator-focused to *participant-centered*. If the group size is fewer than 16 participants, adjust the number of questions to two or three.

> Here's how "snowballing" works. You'll have about three minutes to discuss each question. I'll keep time and tell you when to begin the next step.

> First, find a partner to discuss Question 1. When I say "begin," share ideas with each other for about three minutes. Then, I'll say, "time to snowball" and the two of you will join another pair (you will now have four people in your group) and discuss Question 2.

> After three more minutes, I'll say, "time to snowball," and your group of four will join another group of four (you will now have eight people in your group) and discuss Question 3. Then, after three more minutes, I'll say, for the last time, "time to snowball," and the eight of you will join another group of eight. Are there any questions?

Have a watch with a second hand or set the timer on your phone. Ask participants to find a partner to discuss Question 1. Say, "begin," and monitor the flow of discussion (pairs usually take the shortest time).

After about three minutes, say "Time to snowball," and, if needed, help pairs find another pair to discuss Question 2, and so on, following the directions above. Facilitate the activity in a less structured way so that participants have ownership and control. The facilitator's role is to adjust the timing to keep the pace lively, to provide guidance and support when needed, and to encourage full participation.

At the end of the session, reconvene the group. Ask for their feedback on snowballing as a technique. Help the group make the transition back to the facilitator-focused group through brief discussion and summary statements.

Note

An alternative to using the snowballing technique, which works best with a large group is to have a total group discussion using the questions. Read (or ask for a volunteer to read) the *Questions on ways to develop your organization's multicultural competence* slide (S15).

Facilitate a brief discussion using these questions:

> 1. What did you learn about other agencies' efforts to develop multicultural competence?
>
> 2. Based on the ideas generated, can you name one way in which you could help your agency enhance its cultural competence?

12. Interagency collaboration (30 min.)

In advance of this activity, post easel paper with a marker at four stations around the room. Write one of the following statements on each sheet:

1. Ways to learn about an organization's structure, leadership, learning, and social norms

2. Ways to develop formal and informal relationships between new collaborators

3. Guidelines for sharing information and communicating with partners

4. Examples of conflicts that occur in interagency collaborations

Introduce this topic and activity with a statement such as:

> By working together on projects and initiatives, agency staff members learn to respect each other's cultures as they study issues, make decisions, set goals, and provide services collaboratively.

> Interagency collaboration is seldom simple; it is often one of the most challenging aspects of leadership. However, interagency collaborations provide tremendous opportunities to bridge gaps in support for families and to make efficient use of funding and resources.

> Systems-level collaborations can help promote changes in agencies approaches from deficit-oriented to empowerment-based.

> Carmen and Yvette's vignette in Chapter 5 describes how differences in organizational cultures can influence the dynamics of an interagency collaboration. The vignette in the chapter portrayed their reactions to each other and their perceptions of how to proceed with the collaboration during their first meeting.

> Here is a hypothetical dialogue of their second meeting.

Distribute the *Carmen and Yvette's second meeting* handout (H10). Ask for two volunteers to read the dialogue.

> Using the information from the first vignette (refer to p. 125 in the book) and now the dialogue from the second meeting, we'll brainstorm ideas for developing a successful collaboration. We'll use the rotating stations discussion technique. Choose one of the four stations posted around the room to begin this exercise.

Ask participants to go to the station of their choice. This technique allows participants to self-select their discussion group. Encourage them to join with people they haven't worked with before.

If the stations are poorly balanced, ask for volunteers to join or leave those stations so there is a balance of participants in discussion. Thank participants who are willing to switch groups.

> As a group, keep the vignette in mind and write down ideas in response to the statement on the easel paper. After a few minutes I'll ask all the groups to rotate to the next station. Each group will review the ideas offered by the previous group. Your group can build on those ideas or add new ones.

After a few minutes, I'll ask the groups to rotate again until all groups have visited each station. When your group gets to the last station, designate a spokesperson to present ideas on the newsprint to the larger group. Are there any questions?

When groups are ready, let them begin. Allow three to five minutes for brainstorming, then ask the groups to rotate to the next station. Continue the rotation until all groups have visited the four stations. When they reach the last station, visit each group and ask them to designate a spokesperson.

When it is time for the spokespersons to report, do one of the following: ask participants to stay together at their station throughout the report time, ask all participants to travel from station to station, or ask them sit while you travel from station to station.

Facilitate a brief discussion using this question:

> **If you could share advice in one sentence on developing a successful interagency collaboration, what would it be?**

H10 Carmen and Yvette's second meeting

Yvette: Jan, our executive director, is very excited about this project. She's hoping we can start training as soon as possible. The fiscal officer at my agency said the grant award is in place, and as soon as training begins, we can submit a voucher for the first benchmark.

Carmen: I presented the idea at our last department meeting, but the comptroller was concerned about the timing. She said that if we don't have agency commitments to guarantee full enrollment right now, we should hold off until we're certain.

Yvette: I've been promoting the course with our supervisors and frontline staff members as well as with our collaborators in other programs. I'm even trying to figure out how we can train some of our administrative support staff. I'm sure things will work out for us.

Carmen: I'm optimistic too, and I appreciate your enthusiasm. But things are more complicated for my agency. Some departments already have a lot of mandatory meetings and in-services. There are staff members who are really hesitant to be out of the office because work piles up so fast. Frontline supervisors need to arrange coverage for workers in training. Even details such as which workers get trained first, mileage allocations, comp time, and potential overtime costs need to be factored in before we can make a commitment to the project.

Yvette: I hadn't looked at it from your point of view. I understand better now. I've been keeping a list of agencies that are interested in sending staff members based on my conversations. How about if I send you the list?

Carmen: Great. While I'm waiting to hear from supervisors about which workers are interested, I can start to work out the rest of the details. It won't happen overnight, but if you can get commitments from your agency and others that would address our enrollment concerns, then I can work on getting my agency completely on board.

Yvette: Thanks, Carmen. You are a great organizer.

Carmen: You've got terrific energy, and I'm looking forward to us working together.

13. The Family Development Leadership Model (20–30 min.)

Introduce this discussion with a statement such as:

> Supervision and leadership in today's society presents a challenge to create an organizational culture that is reflective of the empowered workplace. It is most challenging when it requires changing a well-established power structure based on ingrained attitudes and behaviors. Organizations must continually respond to influences and events around them. In essence, organizations are always changing because leaders, supervisors and staff members are always learning and changing.

> This graphic illustrates how the components align to create this new organizational culture. Each circle represents a chapter we discussed and includes some of the skills and competencies needed to create and lead an empowered workplace.

Review the *Family Development Leadership Model* slide (S16), or distribute it as a handout (H11). It can also be referenced in their book (p. 130). Then continue:

> Of course, the process of changing your organization's culture does not always follow a predictable pattern as it is shown in the graphic.

Conclude with a brief discussion using these questions:

1. How does this framework help you to think about the process of creating an empowered workplace?

2. Where do you feel your organization is in the process?

H11 The Family Development Leadership Model

Leading an Empowered Workplace (*Learning*)

- Empowerment-based training
- Shared power
- Understanding the family development process for staff members and the organization
- Recognizing staff's strengths and natural assets

Workplace Inclusiveness (*Reframing*)

- Respecting individual and collective cultures
- Promoting cultural competence and cultural humility
- Developing multicultural competence in interagency collaboration
- Creating a new organizational culture using the Family Development Model

The Empowered Supervisor and Leader

Transforming Your Workplace through Empowerment-Based Leadership (*Realigning*)

- Empowering, compassionate support
- Aligning leadership vision with mission
- Building agency capacity for transformation
- "Talking the talk," "walking the walk"
- Outcomes-based assessment and collaboration

Supervising with Skill and Heart (*Negotiating*)

- Developing bifocal and peripheral vision, and reflecting-in-action
- Building workplace relationships
- Understanding group dynamics
- Handling workplace stress, burnout, and trauma
- Reframing and "I" messages
- Handling conflict
- Creative discussion and facilitation

Leadership and Self-Empowerment (*Reflecting*)

- Principles of empowerment-based leadership and assessment
- Developing a personal vision
- Effective leadership and supervision
- Mindfulness
- Stress reduction
- Personal health, wellness

14.   Sharing the Leadership Empowerment Plans (time is class-size dependent)

Note

At the previous session, instructors should have spent some time discussing the Leadership Empowerment Plan, which is part of the FDC Leadership Portfolio. Leaders set a goal reflecting the concepts taught throughout the course. It should be a realistic and practical plan using a real challenge or task they would like to address over the next month or in the near future.

One option might be to develop steps to incorporate a stronger empowerment-based philosophy or approach within their organization. The goal they decide on should be meaningful and relevant to their individual workplace. Peer Advisors work with each other to develop their plans as they did with the Independent Learning Projects for each chapter.

At the conclusion of the course, invite each leader to share their Leadership Empowerment Plan with the group including any reflections on progress made. Depending on the size of the group, establish a time frame in advance (for example, five to ten minutes per person). If the group is large, we suggest scheduling a separate session for sharing the Leadership Empowerment Plans that could be combined with a final celebration. The time frame and scheduling are up to the instructor and what works best for the group.

Sharing their Leadership Empowerment Plans enhances the networking and supportive connections that have developed throughout the course that will hopefully continue in the future.

15. Planning Independent Learning Projects (30 min.)

Invite participants to spend a few minutes thinking about another project that will demonstrate what they have learned in this chapter.

Ask them to find a partner with whom they will alternate the role of peer advisor and advisee. Ask them to get together and spend some time each discussing their plans. Encourage them to support each other in setting a manageable plan and time frame to complete their projects.

16. Final Feedback Form (10 min.)

In advance, make copies of the final feedback form to distribute at the end of the session

Thank people for their time and their participation in coming to the course. Ask them to complete the "Empowerment Skills for Leaders Final Feedback" form.

Gathering the group together in a circle, briefly share ways in which the course has helped you appreciate the strengths and challenges that supervisors and leaders encounter. Allow participants to share their thoughts on what the series has meant to them. A meaningful closing activity, or ceremony with light refreshments, can provide a thoughtful and uplifting way to end the course.

Empowerment Skills for Leaders
Final Feedback Form

1. What about this course was most useful to you?

_____

_____

_____

2. What did you learn or realize?

_____

_____

_____

3. What would you have changed, if you could, about the way the course was offered, or about how the ideas were presented?

_____

_____

_____

4. What's one thing you think you might do differently as a result of this course?

_____

_____

_____

5. Any other thoughts or suggestions? (Please use the reverse side of this sheet, if needed.)

_____

_____

_____

Thank you for your feedback.

Chapter 5 PowerPoint slides

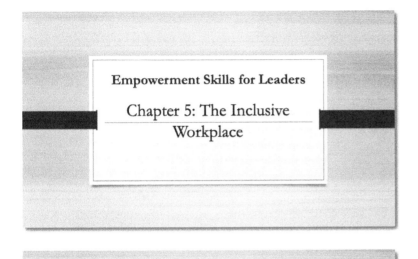

Empowerment Skills for Leaders

Chapter 5: The Inclusive Workplace

Chapter 5: Learning Objectives

* Practice the skills necessary to develop increased cultural humility and inclusiveness in the workplace.
* Understand the benefits and challenges of multiculturalism in a changing American society.
* Explore elements of your personal cultural identity.
* Take steps to strengthen cultural sensitivity and inclusiveness in the workplace.

S1

Learning Objectives (continued)

* Identify aspects of your agency's organizational culture.
* Recognize barriers to achieving multicultural competence and inclusiveness in the workplace.
* Understand how differences in organizational culture may impact collaboration efforts.
* Develop and implement a Leadership Empowerment Plan encompassing the strengths-based principles of family development.

S1

Definition of culture in a family development context

Culture is a body of human behaviors, customs, beliefs and social forms that may be found in distinct social, racial, religious or ethnic groups. These behaviors are embodied in thought, speech, actions, and artifacts, and are dependent on the capacity for learning and transmitting knowledge to succeeding generations.

S2

Multiculturalism Is

➢ A way to understand personal experience in the context of the larger culture.

➢ Based on respect for all cultures and personal accountability for our views

➢ Proposes that personal experience is a valuable way to learn how to honor and respect other cultures.

S3

Definition of cultural competence

Cultural competence is the ability to learn from and relate respectfully to people of your own culture, as well as those from other cultures. It includes adjusting your behaviors based on what you learn. Cultural competence is not a skill that once mastered, remains static. It is a life-long process.

S4

Cultural Humility

- Recognizes cultural competence as a process, not an end.
- Goes beyond cultural competence when mere knowledge is not enough, delving deeper into self-reflection.
- Promotes a lifelong commitment to self-evaluation and self-critique.
- Acknowledges power imbalances between groups in society.
- Affirms the need for individuals, groups and organizations to model and advocate for systemic change.

S5

Excerpt from the poem "On Caring" by Milton Mayeroff

To care for another person
I must be able to understand them
and their world, as if I were inside it.

I must be able to see, as it were,
with their eyes what their world
is like to them and how they see themselves.

I must be able to be with them in their world,
going into their world in order to
sense from insight what life is like for them,
what they are striving to be,
and what they require to grow.

S6

Historical influences in our lifetime

- The Vietnam War
- The Civil Rights movement
- The Women's movement
- The HIV and AIDS epidemic
- Economic recessions of 1980's and 2008
- War in the Middle East

- 9/11 and terrorism
- Technology growth
- The "Me Too" movement
- Mass shootings and gun violence
- Heroin and opioids epidemic
- Climate change and natural disasters

S7

"Melting pot" or "Salad bowl"

Acculturation is the process whereby newcomers assume some of the cultural attributes of the dominant culture (i.e. learning English, dressing in jeans and T-shirts)

Assimilation is the process of becoming fully incorporated into the social networks of the dominant culture (i.e. giving up cultural customs and traditions, joining a new religious community)

S8

Public aspects of organizational culture

✓ Agency name

✓ Motto or slogan

✓ Programs and services

✓ Organizational structure

✓ Location/building

✓ Brochure/website

✓ Mission statement

✓ Advertisements

✓ Symbols

✓ Events

✓ Others?

S9

Private aspects of organizational culture

✓ Organizational norms (unspoken rules and habits i.e. acceptable attire)

✓ Philosophy

✓ Workplace culture

✓ Values

✓ Morale

✓ Informal learning and development opportunities

✓ Leadership styles

✓ Inter-departmental relationships

✓ Others?

S10

Definition of organizational cultural competence and inclusiveness

Organizational cultural competence and inclusiveness is the *collective* ability of leaders/supervisors and staff members to learn from and relate respectfully to those from other organizational cultures.

Why do leaders, supervisors and staff members all need to work together to develop their organization's cultural competence?

S11

Guidelines for developing your organization's cultural competence and cultural humility

❑Recognize strengths in all cultures (leaders, supervisors, staff members, collaborators, supporters, funders, families).

❑Respect organizational cultural differences.

❑Use cultural knowledge to design and provide services.

❑Reduce or eliminate barriers to organizational cultural competence and cultural humility.

S12

Barriers to organizational cultural competence and cultural humility

Workplace privilege- benefits, freedoms or other advantages given to leaders and supervisors that workers and staff members perceive as special incentives or unilateral "perks".

Workplace prejudice- expressing or promoting opinions, attitudes, and judgements about a leader, supervisor or staff member based on stereotypes, incomplete or inaccurate information.

S13

Barriers to organizational cultural competence and cultural humility (continued)

Workplace discrimination- acting on prejudice in an overt or covert way.

Workplace oppression- using personal, positional or organizational power to deny or interfere with an employee's ability to achieve goals of career advancement and healthy self-reliance.

S13

Ways to develop organizational multicultural competence (humility)

* When planning or beginning a new collaboration or partnership, consider the potential differences in structure, leadership, learning and social norms among the organizational cultures of your partners.

* Early in the collaboration, provide some time for supervisors and staff members from partnering agencies to get to know each other in formal and informal settings.

S14

Ways to develop organizational multicultural competence (humility) (continued)

* Establish guidelines and procedures regarding routine communication among partners including what information is communicated to whom, by whom, and how and when it is shared.

* If conflict surrounding differences in organizational cultures arises, use the steps to resolving conflict and work toward creative solutions.

S14

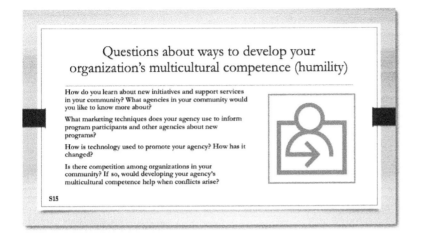

Questions about ways to develop your organization's multicultural competence (humility)

How do you learn about new initiatives and support services in your community? What agencies in your community would you like to know more about?

What marketing techniques does your agency use to inform program participants and other agencies about new programs?

How is technology used to promote your agency? How has it changed?

Is there competition among organizations in your community? If so, would developing your agency's multicultural competence help when conflicts arise?

S15

The Family Development Leadership Model

The Empowered Supervisor and Leader

S16